NEVERTHELESS

The Varieties and Shortcomings
of
Religious Pacifism

John Howard Yoder

Revised and Expanded Edition

HERALD PRESS
Scottdale, Pennsylvania
Waterloo, Ontario

Library of Congress Cataloging-in-Publication Data
Yoder, John Howard.
    Nevertheless : the varieties and shortcomings of religious
pacifism / John H. Yoder. — Rev. and expanded ed.
        p. cm.
    Includes bibliographical references (p.   ) and
index.
    ISBN 0-8361-3586-5 (acid-free)
    1. Pacifism—Religious aspects—Christianity. 2. Historic peace
churches—Doctrines. 3. Just war doctrine. I. Title.
BT 736.4.Y629 1992
327.1'72—dc20   91-39633
                                                           CIP

The paper used in this publication is recycled and meets the minimum
requirements of American National Standard for Information
Sciences—Permanence of Paper for Printed Library Materials, ANSI
Z39.48-1984.

NEVERTHELESS

Related Works by John H. Yoder

"*Christ and Culture:* A critique of H. Richard Niehbur." Available from the Library of Associated Mennonite Biblical Seminaries, Elkhart, Ind.

Christian Attitudes to War, Peace, and Revolution: A Companion to Bainton. Elkhart, Ind.: Goshen Biblical Seminary, 1983.

The Christian and Capital Punishment. Newton, Kan.: Faith and Life Press, 1961, out of print (OP).

The Christian Pacifism of Karl Barth. Washington, D.C.: Church Peace Mission, 1964, OP.

The Christian Witness to the State. Faith and Life Press, 1964, 1977.

A Declaration on Peace: In God's People the World's Renewal Has Begun. Douglas Gwyn, George Hunsinger, Eugene F. Roop, John H. Yoder, eds. Scottdale, Pa.: Herald Press, 1990.

He Came Preaching Peace. Herald Press, 1985, OP; Ann Arbor: Books on Demand, University Microfilms International.

Karl Barth and the Problem of War. Nashville: Abingdon Press, 1970, OP.

The Original Revolution. Herald Press, 1971, OP.

The Politics of Jesus. Grand Rapids: Eerdmans, 1972.

"Reinhold Niebuhr and Christian Pacifism." *Mennonite Quarterly Review* 29 (1955): 101-117.

The Priestly Kingdom: Social Ethics as Gospel. Notre Dame, Ind.: Notre Dame University Press, 1984.

What Would You Do? A Serious Answer to a Standard Question. Herald Press, 1983.

When War Is Unjust: Being Honest in Just-War Thinking. Minneapolis: Augsburg Fortress Press, 1984.

Gratefully Dedicated

To the many friends,
some still militant and some triumphant,
whose different styles of pacifist commitment
have judged and enriched my own.

Contents

Foreword

This is a tremendously helpful and timely book. The Christian discussing pacifism ought to know something about the various types of pacifism, and here one can learn a great deal.

In this new edition John Howard Yoder has revised and expanded the original (1971) publication. To the seventeen major types of pacifism included in the first edition, Yoder has added four more, including "The Pacifism of Rabbinic Monotheism." Thus with the eight types covered only briefly (chapter 17) in both editions, the reader is confronted with twenty-nine clearly distinguished arguments against war.

These types are not presented as being mutually exclusive. Indeed, the pacifist reader will be surprised at how many types one finds within oneself, and the nonpacifist reader may be surprised that there are so many ways of arguing against war.

The book is generously sprinkled with the kind of new and refreshing insights many readers have come to expect from this author.

From high school classes to sophisticated academic debate, discussions about war could profit greatly by using the typology of this book. Communication will be improved as varieties of pacifism are identified by name and the strengths and weaknesses of various positions are honestly debated.

Nevertheless is also a study guide usable beyond its own argument. The footnotes and appendices include a tremendous wealth of bibliographical information, guiding the serious inquirer to some of the most cogent writings available on the subject of war and peace.

At a moment in history when the church is challenged as never before to demonstrate an alternative to power politics and slaughter by technology, I am pleased to commend this book to the reader.

> —*John K. Stoner*
> *Coordinator, New Call to Peacemaking*
> *Former Executive Secretary, U.S. Peace Section*
> *Mennonite Central Committee*
> *Advent 1991*

Preface

One of the constants of serious discussion about the Christian's participation in war is the nagging awareness left with the observer that the parties are talking past each other. This mutual misunderstanding is conditioned partly by simple ignorance. Certain major Christian pacifist traditions have few adherents. Some of them have not been articulated in "mainstream" terms which interlocutors outside of their community can understand fairly. Misunderstanding may also be part of each thinker's personal history, as when Karl Barth and Emil Brunner reacted negatively and emotionally in the 1920s to the pacifism of their former close associate Leonhard Ragaz. In the 1930s, another example of this is Reinhold Niebuhr rejecting the pacifism of the Fellowship of Reconciliation, of which he had been a member.

Some such failure to mesh with the debate is a normal trait whenever there is any major difference. But must the parties be this far apart?

The purpose of this book is to bring some clarity to the many-sided conversation about war which the escalation of armament, the nuclear arms race, the Vietnam and Persian Gulf wars, and other hostilities have helped to open in recent decades. There is need for far greater awareness that "pacifism" is not just one specific position, spoken for authoritatively by just one thinker. Instead, it is a wide gamut of views that vary and are sometimes even contradictory. Rather than plunging ahead to debate right or wrong, we must therefore understand each position seriously for what it says and assumes. That is better than supposing that we can fairly and adequately grasp a stance by assuming that the label it has been given has only one meaning.[1]

I must begin, then, by classifying the various positions to which current labels actually already refer. There is no such thing as a single position called pacifism, to which one clear definition can be given and which is held by all pacifists. Instead, there are varied kinds of opposition to war. Some of them run parallel to each other, but some are quite different from one another in accent and sometimes even in substance. They can be grouped together under the same label only by doing violence to one or the other.

What I am undertaking is thus a *typology*, asking how many different types of pacifism there are and how they differ from one another. Alternatively, we could call it a *topology*, an effort somehow to place the various positions on the map. Or we could call it a *taxonomy*, describing the various phenomena in terms of a kind of order into which we think they fit. Some "pacifisms" are near neighbors and some are distant from each other. In their relations to each other, we must seek to look at each in its own logical right before leaping ahead to an evaluation. I shall not glibly assign to one position or to all of them the flaws one can see in one particular variety.

The concern to perceive each position in its integrity will override even our concern for clarity of analysis. I could have made the job easier for both myself and my readers by fitting the types of pacifism into the ready-made slots of the academic ethicists. I could play moralities of means off against moralities of ends, principles versus intuition, conscience versus responsibility, vision versus judgment, character versus rules, motivations versus strategy. I have no objection if the reader sees such classical systematic-ethical themes showing through, and I shall not hesitate to borrow as shorthand some of these labels where they fit.

I have, however, chosen not to derive my outline by posing such contrasts. Those who set up alternatives in that way nearly always assume that there is but one basic question and but two possible answers to it; thus they let this polarity dominate all analysis. Yet most often it would be more fair to make room for at least three or four choices. Furthermore, such bipolar analysis usually covertly favors one of the two styles. Here I want each position to spring from its own roots. I therefore refuse to sanction any one traditional ethical polarity by pretending that it clarifies and categorizes more than the others.

It may be possible farther along to classify the types and note their intrinsic interlockings, parallels, and overlaps.[2] First, though, I must discern and report their diversity, discovering the integrity and the coherence of each. I shall proceed more or less in the order of decreasing familiarity.

The classification proposed below might not be recognized by all of the persons described. Many pacifists are activist and not given to systematic conceptual analysis. Given individuals or agencies may combine more than one of these positions within their own conviction. Labeling different positions and noticing the differences between them does not necessarily mean that the borders between them are airtight, as we shall see more fully after the survey. Yet this possibility of overlapping does not justify placing all these positions in one sack or accusing those who hold one position of the axioms of another.[3]

Some may read this promenade through the gallery of moral styles as a way to let conceptual analysis throw more light on concrete choices. That will be fine; it is my hope that this review will help readers to think more intelligently about war as a moral issue. Yet the agenda is larger than that. The usefulness of the exercise may flow the other way as well.

The case of war, about which everyone has ideas, provides an excellent opportunity for us to think far more broadly about method in Christian ethics. It helps us think about how our ability to reason morally depends on our usually untested assumptions about the logic of our arguments. The concrete debate may throw further light on questions of logic. For that reason, I shall occasionally insert parenthetical discussions between the "type" descriptions. These sections, not numbered like the other chapters, reflect on what the debate shows us about how we think.

The larger agenda includes as well a need to think more carefully about the values and the pitfalls of pluralism in modern culture. For some, the recognition of variety undercuts the ability to think decisively, or forbids our taking firm positions. The point of this book is to show that that need not be the case.

I gratefully acknowledge important assistance from S. David Garber and Mark Nation in the 1992 revision of this work. John Rempel was never properly thanked for his assistance with the last phases of editing the 1972 edition.

—*John Howard Yoder*
  University of Notre Dame
  Notre Dame, Indiana

1

The Pacifism of Christian Cosmopolitanism

The true and solid peace of nations consists not in equality of arms, but in mutual trust alone.
—Pope John XXIII, *Pacem in Terris*

To understand one way the church may be concerned about peace in the world, we may well begin with the picture of a church in a small town. The Christian church and its pastor in the village will be concerned not only for the thoughts and behavior of the active members of the congregation, but also for the total life of the community. The church will be concerned for the needs and behavior of nonmembers; they will be recognized as neighbors, and their action influences the community atmosphere, for which the church and its leaders will be concerned.

The pastor will not only teach the faithful but also preach to the rest of the community that it is both desirable and generally possible for neighbors to live together in peace. Should there be disputes between neighbors— and not only if they are church members—the small-town pastor will admonish the participants to get together, negotiate, and be reconciled. The pastor will not necessarily take sides nor seek to judge between them. Pastoral guidance will appeal to mature neighborly understanding, without judging the merits of any particular conflict.

In this small town there may be a sheriff, who may carry arms and sometimes use them. But most of the time the reason neighbors live together in peace is not because there is a sheriff. Instead, as intelligent and mature human beings, most of them realize that it is usually in the interest of most of them to make reconciliation and mutual respect the foundation of their social relations. This understanding motivates them to keep the peace, even at the cost of some sacrifice and some accommodation. The Christians have further reason for peaceful living, and the pastor has further reasons for calling for peace, but these reasons generally coincide with the wholesome interest of the whole community.

Now stretch the picture to the worldwide scale. Christians are learning to think globally. This is partly the result of technology, but also partly an effect of the gospel. The church exists, even though feebly, all around the world. Church leaders recognize a responsibility for the whole world as their parish. If the world is the parish, then the church needs to work on the world level in the society of nations to apply the picture of the community which ought to get along together without violence most of the time. The local society must outgrow being governed by feuds and mafia. The border between the United States and Canada is peaceful in the absence of armament rather than because of armament. Just so, on the world level the nations should learn to get along together.

The most striking statements of this position have been those of the popes. Such teaching in the twentieth century can be traced through Benedict XV (1914-22), expanding especially in recent decades with the encyclical *Peace on*

Earth of Pope John XXIII,[1] and culminating symbolically with the 1965 speech of Paul VI at the United Nations.[2] The pope does not assume that all people of goodwill are Christian. Instead, in the name of God, morality, and humanity, he speaks even to non-Christians about what constitutes well-being for everyone in his parish, the world.

The pope does not begin with the fundamental question of the morality of war, nor does he attempt to decide in a given conflict which party is in the right. He simply says in a pastoral way that if people are ever going to get along together, squabbling is no help. This type of moral concern is an expression of the pastoral attitude of the church toward all of society, including unbelievers. In other words, it is a test and an expression of the genuine catholicity (universality) which the church claims. The church confirms, by so speaking, that it is not a national or a provincial community.

Thus in a broad sense we could call this a "catholic" position. Yet it is not unique to the Church of Rome. Many Protestant and Orthodox Christians, some spokespersons for other religions, and secular world federalists hold the same kind of position. The same stance is also being taken increasingly by the World Council of Churches, and other nonreligious dispensers of moral insight can take it as well. It is quite possible logically to speak and to work against war as an institution without taking on the role of adjudicating all differences or imposing the right answers.

The Self-Evident Axiom

The axiom underlying this approach is that our common humanity is both a fact and a moral imperative. Human community—on every scale from village to globe—both needs and authorizes certain voices to speak for "the peace of the city." This is a value in its own right, quite apart from weighing the merits of particular conflicts or particular systems of ethical judgment on the morality of killing. Any church or council which sees the world whole, will today take that shepherd's stance.

The strength of this approach on the part of the church is symbolized by Pope Paul's visit to the United Nations, or by the epoch-making first visit of Soviet President Podgorny to Rome soon after that. There is a kind of real moral authority which a person or an institution can carry, and it can demand and get a serious hearing from society at large. This is not a constitutional right; it holds true only at certain times and places and on certain subjects. Nevertheless, it is a reality to reckon with. Society can be helped in specific cases by the ways in which bearers of moral authority identify issues and apply the weight of their prestige. This can happen apart from any change in the religious commitment of individuals, and without any formal recognition of that moral authority by any public agency.

Shortcomings

If we measure this kind of catholic pacifism by the standards of Christian moral theology, it has some real shortcomings. Does it not give to society at large the idea that Christianity is basically a set of moral teachings which can be understood independently of their rootage in the faith? It suggests that those teachings are sometimes opposed to the true interest and welfare of people, and practically impossible to live up to; for the world to listen, they need to be reduced to something less demanding. Teaching such an understanding of moral demands implies to some hearers that these demands can be met with human resources alone. It gives to others an impression of irrelevance. Can moral exhortation thus speak of what is generally good for society while sidestepping firm commitment on contested matters of morality, such as whether killing itself is ever wrong?

Earlier churchly expressions of this concern were the medieval institutions of the Peace of God and the Truce of God. Bishops in the Middle Ages sought to limit war to certain times and certain places.[3] This legitimized feudal war backhandedly in the course of efforts to limit it. Might not this modern display of pastoral concern without ethical rigor also undercut its own real intent?

Another general weakness is that this kind of moral authority is easily discredited where it has been called on too often and not heard. Where war is likely or is already being waged, such admonition cannot stop the fighting. It cannot prevent the explosion of hostilities where men or nations have already ceased to think of one another as belonging to the same society.[4]

Such a pastoral concern for all the world can also fail to take sides when the truth does demand a recognition that both parties are not equally to blame.[5]

Nevertheless

Even with all of the serious shortcomings, this catholic or pastoral peace concern is still morally superior to any of the various types of religious provincialism which are the only alternatives to it. With such provincialism, a church identifies with and thereby morally absolutizes a given nation. The church thereby renounces the possibility of standing in judgment over that province or nation for turning against all the world. Therefore, religious provincialism is subject to all the same weaknesses just mentioned, and in addition it abandons the world orientation.

Whenever war actually breaks out, it eats away at existing communities. In order to pursue the Vietnam War, the United States contributed to the breakdown of NATO. To back up its invasions threatened in Cuba and actual in the Dominican Republic, then more recently in Nicaragua, Grenada, and Panama, the United States decreased its loyalty to the decision-making power of the Organization of American States, and to the Court of International Justice at the Hague. Thus a war is not only against a particular enemy people. Each war also destroys a wider fabric of community.

After All

Even the most convinced advocate of military violence still applies this inclusive "catholic" attitude within his own country. The Pentagon would not approve of having armies along both sides of the Potomac River and along every state line as the only way to keep the peace among the fifty states. Such a renunciation of violence between the several provinces of a nation is taken for granted even by the military. So the real issue is not whether it is possible or wise to renounce violence within a given realm but whether the realm in question must necessarily be the nation or could possibly be a larger segment of the world.

The Pentagon agrees that war is wrong between Arizona and California or between the Southern States and New England, or even between the United States and Canada, or even Mexico. By not preparing for such war, the Pentagon assures that it will not happen. The only question on which the Pentagon and the pacifists differ is the size of the community within which internal warfare is wrong.

What made peace possible or war impossible between Pennsylvania and New Jersey was not that one of them finally won a war against the other. The maintenance of peace by that means tends with time to foster further fragmentation. We have just seen since 1990 the breakup of nations (e.g., Yugoslavia) and empires (e.g., USSR) previously held together only by conquest. What made permanent peace possible between two states in the American commonwealth was their recognition of an already given commonality. They accepted that on a scale far broader and on a level far deeper than legal territorial limits.

But Christians are by definition committed to positing as their homeland the larger commonality of humankind, rather than the territorial unit. Thus the prerequisites for not needing war are present. Any disorder is a family offense to be dealt with by adjustments within the framework of mutual acceptance, not on the model of a clan conflict or the repression of the outsider.

2

The Pacifism of the Honest Study of Cases

Some decades ago war may have been an instrument which, although it was brutal, could be used to resolve intolerable international tension; but today, owing to the fact that it cannot be controlled, it has lost even this shred of utility. . . . It has become so colossal that it can no longer exercise any sensible function.
—Emil Brunner, *The Divine Imperative*

Part of any honestly disciplined approach to ethical decision employs what is technically called casuistry, the application of one's general moral orientation to particular decisions. With regard to the problem of war, there is an ancient tradition whose purpose (not necessarily the same as its achievement) has been to do just this. It looks case by case at every possible war, to distinguish between those purely wrong and those perhaps justifiable.

Such a position does not grant that war is always right. That would be to sell out morally to whatever a given government wants to do. Nor does this position believe that it is possible for the church to call upon the state to help the church in its theological concerns by waging a holy war or crusade. To be honest, we can at most say, according to this line of thought, that war might sometimes be justifiable. This then obligates us to study in detail the characteristics of a particular case in which that would be true. We must evaluate the cause for which a war is fought, the authority in whose name it is undertaken, and the methods used.

The Axiom

Underlying so-called just-war pacifism is the axiom that every ethical decision must be made concretely. One must not sell out in advance, either to the decision made by a government in favor of war, or to an absolute principled pacifism adopted prior to the measurement of the exact form of a given war. Moral integrity is a matter of making one's decisions by applying one's general commitments critically and rigorously to given cases.

If there is no prior commitment to objective standards, one is not morally accountable. Thus the prior public statement of one's standards, and a commitment to their application, does not sacrifice one's freedom to make decisions in the situation. Instead, it is the only safeguard that one can remain free, in the face of a given future pressure for decision, to say no if that is the necessary answer.

This is not the place to describe in detail what the traditionally defined standards of the just-war theory have been nor the style of their application. It is sufficient for our purposes to recognize that if this process of moral evaluation of a particular war or weapon is honest, it must at least sometimes be possible for the conclusion reached to be negative. Just-war adherents would honestly evaluate a war which a given government is waging or wishes to wage. Then occasionally they must reject that war, not on the grounds of general pacifism, but because it is not an acceptable political undertaking even for someone who does not reject all killing.[1]

The new thing in the last forty years, especially the last thirty, is that some persons have been honest enough in their application of those standards to come to negative conclusions. This is shown by their appraisals of the massive city bombings of World War II, of the threat of nuclear war since 1945,[2] and of the murderous meaning of counterinsurgency war since Vietnam. To this we can add the lessons from the Persian Gulf War as to the disproportionate destructiveness of uncontrolled high-tech weapons. We can review the causes for which war is fought, or the authority in whose name it is fought. As a result, we can see some wars today to be imperialistic or aggressive or to have the effect of perpetuating a tyrannical form of government.

When we evaluate methods, certain characteristics of modern war are leading an increasing number of persons to a negative conclusion about its admissibility. Some of these features are the destructiveness and uncontrollability of nuclear weapons, guerrilla and counter-guerrilla methods, especially painful weapons like napalm or guava bombs, biological warfare, carpet bombing, and types of attack which bring suffering especially to noncombatants.

There is nothing new about the fundamental principles behind this position. The doctrine of the just war has been the official position of all western Christian communions since the Crusades, with the exception of a few tiny "peace churches" and a few solitary prophets. All that has changed in recent years is the nature of the wars to which the standards are to be applied.

The quotation from Emil Brunner (originally 1932)[3] is one of the earliest statements of this position within mainstream Christianity. Brunner drew from this reasoning, which he called "genuine pacifism" as contrasted to non-casuistic positions, the justification for a kind of conscientious refusal of war based on the just-war criteria. He was followed in this by Karl Barth, Paul Ramsey, and more recently by many Roman Catholic[4] and Lutheran thinkers.

Shortcomings

This position has numerous logical, theological, and practical weaknesses. Although it seeks seriously to measure good and evil in causes and methods, it has no clear yardstick for this—especially not for weighing one good value against another. How much freedom is worth how many civilian lives? What is a military target? What is a legitimate government? The logic and the theology of this position assume that these questions can all be given neat answers. But in fact none of them can.

A second difficulty is that in many cases, having stated such a doctrine seems to have had the effect of excusing people from applying it carefully. They think the fact that there exists a doctrine of the just war[5] constitutes a justification of war in general. However, it actually constitutes a denial that war can ever be *generally* justified. The amassing of armament for the potentially justified case of war is not matched by creating institutions or techniques for the control of the use of arms in the other cases.

Thus the existence of the doctrine has tended to be taken as a proof, when as a matter of fact it should have been meant as a question. Hence, great numbers of Christians in the mainstream denominations assume that the theologians have given them grounds for a good conscience in preparing for war and waging it. Yet this is not at all the case. They feel that the recent groundswell of selective objection to war is revolutionary, when in fact it is a retrieval of traditional commitments.[6]

From a specifically Christian perspective, a further shortcoming is that holders of just-war doctrine regard the

Christian making a decision about war as being the equivalent of a righteous policeman. They assume that this bearer of "just authority" has the capacity to impose his or her will. So they only ask when it is permitted to use all that power, or how much of it may properly be used when. Thus the entire structure of the doctrine dodges what the New Testament calls the cross. The cross stands for the serious possibility that the only fate for followers of truth or righteousness in a given situation might be crucifixion, defeat, powerlessness.

I have been pointing just now to the internal limitations of the just-war position as a kind of logic. To look at it from the perspective of the nonpacifist, just-war pacifism or selective pacifism can be accused of mixing illegitimately the realms of politics and religion. This is so especially when persons appeal to it as a justification for conscientious-objector status in the face of the draft.

The criteria by which the unjust-war objector[7] measures, in order to conclude that a given war is wrong, are the same as those of political judgment: the legitimacy of a government, of a cause, of the instruments of policy. But then those whom the conscientious objector inconveniences take the objector to be using religious sanction to glorify political dissent.[8] They think the objector merely has a different political view of what constitutes legitimate instruments of policy and is jeopardizing the health of the community by claiming an absolute moral obligation to refuse to support the political decisions of legitimate government.

Nevertheless

This position is still more honest than any of the alternatives available to those who do not reject all war. It does away with the crusade which blesses war, and the fascism which makes the state an autonomous value subject to no criteria of judgment. Saying yes to war, subject to some stated conditions, is morally more responsible than saying yes with no limits. Such a person may apply the conditions seriously to modern war and actually come up with a negative answer. That is more honest than saying there are limits but never reaching them.[9]

This theory recognizes a standard of moral judgment superior to the state. It admits that the instruments of the state must be used only for modest and finite values rather than being put in the service of a crusade. In any orderly type of society other than an outspoken dictatorship, the language of the just-war tradition is one of the most appropriate ways to communicate a Christian peace concern to Christians or to others who claim to be honest politicians.

Outside the historic peace churches, the language of the just-war tradition is a most appropriate vehicle of communication. It is the historic position held at least in theory by all the major Christian bodies. Within this framework, one can ask questions which implicitly lead beyond the limits of the position itself: If you say not all wars are right, what are the standards which you have to identify those which are wrong? What preparation have you made to be in a position to obey the government when it plans a wrong war? Is that preparation comparable to the investment of effort and plans your society has made in being ready to serve in a right one?[10]

To speak against war by means of the language of the just-war tradition is not to impose the Sermon on the Mount on the world. An unjust-war objector uses language and criteria which are of recognized appropriateness in the realm of the state and therefore cannot be brushed off as irresponsible.

Furthermore, this pacifism of borderline casuistry is logically the first step which an individual takes along the path to a more consistent pacifism. First, one might get accustomed to the idea that one might ever say no, and that one might ever apply critical moral criteria to the claims of the government. Only then can one even conceive of a more radical moral independence.[11]

After All

Those who allow themselves to go beyond just-war limits with a given war are still just-war casuists about the enemy. They justify their own intervention by condemning the "aggression" of the adversary. After the war is won, they condemn through judicial process (Nuremberg, Oradour, Eichmann) those leaders on the losing side who failed to disobey their own government. They create or sustain governments in exile which claim legitimacy over against the enemy regime, and they publicize the "atrocities" of the opposing army. All the criteria of just-war logic are implicit in such propaganda. If we reject the restraints which just-war thought would impose upon our own violence, we destroy implicitly the case we make against the enemy for not having observed those same restraints.

Parenthesis: Exceptions and How to Weigh Them

One variation of pacifism might in strict logic be classified with this just-war type. Numerous important interpreters of *pacifism* use that word as an adequate self-designation and reject *all* war, yet do not reject violent personal self-defense, or the violent defense of an innocent third party if in their immediate personal presence. Their reason for rejecting all war may be expressed in any of the numerous different ways which I shall be describing (and distinguishing) in the coming chapters. Yet their reason for accepting violence in this one exceptional close-to-home case is a microcosm of the just-war argument.

This makes the case against war easier to argue. One stereotypical pro-war argument most routinely arises in amateur debate: "Would you not defend your wife or child?"[1] This kind of pacifist cuts that argument off at the ground by saying, "Yes, but war is different." War is different from self-defense, or from local emergency intervention, in many ways, not only in scale.[2] Local self-defense stops the guilty person; not his wife or neighbors. War is prepared for in advance by the development of institutions, budgets, professions, and a culture of hostility. It reaches beyond the realm of a nation's own sovereignty. It destroys positive cultural values (e.g., the public water and sewage system of Baghdad in January 1991) which have nothing to do with the offense.

Some of the strongest voices for pacifism have made room for this exception to the rejection of violence. It was the case for Martin Luther King, Jr., at least in the early years of his public ministry. It was the position of Thomas Merton. It was the position Gandhi took when the issue was put as a choice between cowardice and courage.[3]

A Shortcoming

It may count as a weakness of this view that it sacrifices intellectual rigor, by being willing to make one exception, namely the one closest to home. If the pacifism is founded in a sweeping moral generalization[4] or in a spiritual commitment to loving the enemy and not returning good for evil, then to make an exception at the point closest to home can seem to undercut the entire argument. If you are willing to break a rule in the place where it most prototypically applies, is it still a rule?

Nevertheless

The qualitative distinction between war as a massive institutional phenomenon and personal self-defense is yet undeniable. Practically nothing which war does can in fact be justified on the ground of defending innocent individuals against their being the victims of direct hostile attack. If everyone accepted individual defense but nothing more than that, the reality of war in our time would be done away with. Leaving open the loophole of personal defense of the innocent, in a situation of ethical debate, may be a good move; it corrects for a legalistic or even superstitious notion according to which the fear of bloodshed would be the center.

It may also be argued in favor of this view that it can correct for a scrupulous or wimpish understanding of the Christian position as unassertive.[5] Such a view, as in the notion that assertiveness is a vice, is sometimes held to by people who eschew violence. It is also sometimes wrongly ascribed to them by others. I would defend the innocent victim of an attack;[6] what I deny is that that intention justifies killing the assailant.

Last, it must be pointed out that none of the three major figures named above, who granted the legitimacy of the violent defense of the individual victim, when speaking in theory, is recorded as ever having taken such an action or advocated it in a particular case. This means that the concession, made in order not to seem too rigid in intellectual debate, was not representative. This becomes even more clear when one studies how they undergird their nonviolence with a coherent worldview.[7]

3

The Pacifism of Absolute Principle

> *When God prohibits killing, he not only forbids brigandage, which is not allowed even by the public laws, but he warns us not to do even those things which are legal among men. And so it will not be lawful for a just man to serve as a soldier . . . nor to accuse anyone of a capital offense, because it makes no difference whether you kill with a sword or with a word, since killing itself is forbidden.*
> —Lactantius of Bithynia (ca. 310)

Explore with me what belief in God entails:

- *If* there is a God (rather than "God" being merely a code name to refer to our own best ideas) . . . and
- *If* God reveals himself and his will (rather than merely putting a rubber stamp on our most sincere decisions) . . . and
- *If* we are in real need of this revelation if we are to be saved and guided (with ignorance and a warped will both being characteristics of the unaided—classical theology would say "fallen"—human state) . . .
- *Then* it is logically inevitable that the revealed will of God will be, at least at some points, different in its form and substance from what human beings would otherwise

have thought on the same subject. There must therefore be a limit set to the applicability of human common sense and the right to calculate right and wrong. We must expect that there will be points where the will of God will simply have to be taken on the authority of revelation.

Traditional theology has long seen such *revealed principles* in Scripture. Other moral traditions find them in the speech of prophets and oracles. In current thought, among educated elites in the West in the 1990s, this mode of understanding the origin and content of ethical knowledge is out of style, but it remains a respectable minority position, and still has in its favor the logic cited above. The changes of theological fashion have tried to leave this logic behind, but have never really refuted it.

Hence, if there be such a thing as principles, whether we think we find these expressed in the text of the Ten Commandments or in some other form, it is likely that the sanctity of human life will be one of them.[1] Such a position can be held in puritanical and legalistic ways, but it need not be. It can be quite at home within a sectarian understanding of the place of the church in the world, but it need not be limited to that context. It can be the expression of naive assumptions about how God gave the Ten Commandments to Israel, but need not be.

This position was given its most categorical expression in recent years by the Austrian Roman Catholic theologian Johannes Ude.[2] The command "Thou shalt not kill" is, according to Ude, an absolute which admits of no exceptions. It is on a higher level of authority than the various other political practices and prescriptions in the Old Testament which still left a place for violence.

Long before Ude, however, the notion of law in a New Testament context had a special centrality in the Czech Reformation of the fifteenth century.[3] In the passage of the Sermon on the Mount which began, "Do not think that

I have come to abolish the law or the prophets," Jesus went on to say, "You have heard that it was said. . . . But I say to you. . . ." The Czech Brethren named this guidance "the minor precepts"[4] and, considering Jesus as Lord, set about obeying him. Three of the six precepts have to do with war.[5]

Later cultures, especially Lutheran and existentialist, have put the notion of a morality of law in an unfavorable light; but in the fifteenth century this was an important leverage for moral renewal. It was retrieved as well in the nineteenth century by Tolstoy in the Russian Empire, after Ballou and Garrison in the USA.

The Axiom

Underlying this stance is the belief that we human beings are not capable of saving ourselves. We have to be guided, by meaningful general directives, received from beyond ourselves, and bearing authority over us. *Revelation* is the religious label for that. In a similar way, a nontheistic moral will lean on similarly structured generalizations which will be accepted as derived from reason, human dignity, or the experience of the race.

Shortcomings

However, the pacifism of principle can easily be caricatured by the naive who apply it legalistically, in a self-righteous or self-deceiving way. Libertines exaggerate and ridicule "absolutes"[6] because they are unaware of their own irrational commitments to authorities outside themselves. But this is not a significant shortcoming of the position. Such weak spots are found in every system. Their presence is more a fruit of varying levels of sophistication than of differing ethical postures. They are unavoidable if an ethical posture is to be taken by a whole community, by simple and busy people.

The more serious weaknesses are on the logical level. Even the most categorical command is still communicated in human language and carried by human documents. Whether the documents be the human mind or the Old Testament, the meaning of a verbal command is equivocal, open to two or more interpretations. As people give and receive communication, even if it be in the name of God, the message is subject to shadings of meaning. Many fail to respect those nuances if they have the habit of thinking of a limited number of absolute principles. This is well exemplified by the case of the Ten Commandments where the most precise translation would probably read "Thou shalt commit no murder" rather than "Thou shalt not kill."[7]

The second difficulty of this approach is the problem of collision when more absolutes than one are calling for allegiance in the same situation. Situations of collision of absolutes can easily be imagined or documented from history. It may seem necessary to choose between not lying and not taking life, or between not taking one life and not defending another. The concept of absolute principle does not suffice here.

Still another shortcoming is the negative form which such absolutes almost inevitably must take. The effort to respect such prescriptions easily becomes transformed into a search for moral purity for its own sake, rather than an expression of love of the neighbor. It is possible to be scrupulous about not taking life, and yet lack insight into the positive obligations which flow from a genuine respect for that same life.

Nevertheless

In the serious ethical decision-making process, the language of principled obligation, whatever its practical and philosophical shortcomings, is still the clearest language we have. It is the most reliable in social settings where it keeps the other party to a covenant from bending the rules. The burden of proof still lies with those who claim that it is possible to have a community of moral discourse without certain shared understandings which function somehow like rules.

Situation ethicists speak to the individual's decision-making in a given context. They have much that is wholesome to say about flexibility, about the importance of loving motivation, and about the uniqueness of each choice. But they say this to persons who have already acquired somewhere a set of understandings about what constitutes the neighbor's welfare, with which they can then afford to be flexible. Situation ethicists have not demonstrated how ethical decision can be the subject of community concern without recourse to principle.[8] Some standards are needed in justifying or condemning choices, in nurturing the immature, in adjudicating conflicts between the differing demands of different loves, and in aiding individuals to keep watch on their own hasty and unworthy loves for the sake of longer-range and worthier love of neighbor.

After All

Any case that can be made for war also appeals to principles claiming to stand above the individual. And those principles supporting war are generally less flexible, less humane, and less moral than those appealed to against war. In the concrete conflict situation, we need to weigh the pacifism of absolute principle against other absolutes, equally blunt and oversimplified.

Some of the absolutes used to justify war are courage, comradeship, freedom, a particular preferred form of government, the direction of history, and integrity of territory. When they become reasons for killing, these all are just as absolute in their demands and far less human or humane in the attitude they express. They are more degrading than pacifist absolutes applied in legalistic, self-justifying ways by the naive and those not equipped (as is the situationist) for the luxury of situationally anguished existential choices.

These pagan absolutes function with the same logical weaknesses as those of the Ten Commandments but are far less worthy of such respect. They are more rigid psychologically: who can argue with "better dead than Red"? They are also more rigid institutionally: the provision for killing is self-authenticating and self-governing. The military establishment has to be code-bound in a way that the church does not need to be.

As an absolute, "Thou shalt not kill" is still immeasurably more human, more personalistic, more genuinely responsible than any competitive absolute: "Thou shalt not let Uncle Sam down," "Thou shalt fight for freedom," or "Never give up the ship." In the age of Abraham or Moses, the blanket prohibition of killing freed the Hebrews from the scourge of infant sacrifice. Even so today, such a person-centered absolute prohibition may well help free us from other idolatries.

4

The Pacifism of Programmatic Political Alternatives

Can men practice politics without doing violence? The answer is an imperative: They must if humanity is to live. The fact that some men can do so is evident enough in the struggles of a Hindu ascetic and a Swedish diplomat to lay the basis for the hope that a politics of revolution and peace is within the grasp of many more. To face the cost of such a politics, in the cross, is to affirm simultaneously the resurrection of humanity that is its outcome.
—James Douglass, *The Non-Violent Cross*

We are not so mad as to think that we shall create a world in which murder will not occur. We are fighting for a world in which murder will no longer be legal.
—Albert Camus

The only thing that's been a worse flop than the organization of nonviolence has been the organization of violence.
—Joan Baez

When we speak here of the *political*, we refer to positions being taken or advocated for governments. A political program does not begin with the individual and what he may or may not do. Instead, it starts with decisions which the government must make. Whenever we refer to this political pacifism as programmatic, we indicate that it proposes concrete plans and goals rather than contenting itself with generalizations or condemnations.

Followers of programmatic political pacifism will propose for general adoption the banning of nuclear tests, the strengthening of the United Nations, or progressive disarmament. They will offer intelligent and feasible solutions for problems which war does not solve. They assume that there must be a peaceful solution to any political problem, including the kinds of conflicts others fight about, if competent political thought is directed to it.

The Underlying Axiom

Programmatic political pacifists claim that war is not a solution to any problem. Measured by its worthy announced goals, war is counterproductive. The statesman who resorts to war as an instrument of national policy is shortsighted and selfish. We therefore need to counteract his ignorance and selfishness by supplying concrete suggestions which the statesman or his constituency can responsibly support.

This kind of programmatic pacifism was especially prevalent in Anglo-Saxon countries in the early 1930s. It was widely represented within Protestant churches, even though its reasoning was not specifically religious in origin. On the level of popular acceptance, it largely collapsed in the later thirties with the rise of Hitler and from then on was given little serious attention by mainstream figures. Its most consistent adversaries have been thinkers like Reinhold Niebuhr, who himself had once held such a position.[1]

Shortcomings

Some apparent weaknesses of this position are minor and not constitutive. It is often held by naive people, whose calculation of what is politically possible is not based on realistic knowledge or experience. Further, sometimes a position proposed from this perspective might be technically possible and socially desirable. Yet it generally has little hope of commanding wide support either from the politicians currently in power or from sufficiently wide segments of the population at large.

But there is another set of weaknesses which are more significant. This programmatic pacifism tends to misread the possibilities of wholesome social development. It may place too much confidence in the efficacy of the methods it proposes. It may count too much on the goodwill of the parties in control. Thus, programmatic pacifists may consider as feasible certain strategies which actually have no hope of effectiveness, however desirable the goals might otherwise be, and however appropriate the method might intrinsically be.

By thus overestimating the likelihood of healthy solutions, this programmatic pacifism does not face outright the problem of failure. In its concern to propose a feasible alternative, it may concede to the power politicians their assumption that only guaranteed-to-be-feasible alternatives are morally binding. It may accept that morality should properly be tested by the promise of sure results. Does the tacit acceptance of such a test not open the door to authorizing violence after all, if no other alternative works out? Or can the moral deed sometimes be the ineffective and costly thing?

To face this latter challenge in a Christian way, pacifism needs a rootage in the meaning of the cross of Christ. The way Jesus took certainly was not a visibly effective strategy for reaching any worthwhile shortrange political goal.[2]

Nevertheless

Yet this sober pessimism about the usability of force and this creativity as to human solutions is what (all agree[3]) is needed in most societies, and even in most international conflicts, most of the time. Differing therein from the utopian or sectarian forms of pacifism, as well as from the utopian claims of militarism (see below), programmatic pacifism does accept the challenge of realism and relevance.[4] Such pacifists make a convincing condemnation of trust in weapons by arguing that without weapons, one could meet some of the same needs and achieve some worthy ends. They do not abandon society to be condemned along with the world's militarism.

Programmatic pacifism can afford, as the alternatives cannot, to be sober about the destructive potential inherent in the appeal to arms, and the likelihood of failure to achieve the set goals. Every war has a loser on one side, and sometimes both lose, when measured by the beginning goals. These pacifists, by not resorting to the simple solution of violence and thereby cutting short the creative search for real solutions, force themselves to stay by the problem until they find another way through.[5]

If the claims of this programmatic approach are to be given a fair hearing, then we must project applications which would draw on the same resources in money, planning, and potential sacrifice of life which war can claim.[6] "Nonviolence has never worked" is not a logically honest argument, when in fact it has never been tried.

There has never been a serious mobilization for nonviolence, with planning, strategy thinking, and education like the military does, with budget for strategic studies and training, with investment in building skills and esprit de corps, and with readiness to sacrifice lives in the struggle. Let us measure by such a fair test, in proportion to the cost of military methods in preparation and in lives. Suppose there were such a thing as a calculus of units-of-justice-per-cost-in-persons. Then one could certainly argue that history's few, hastily projected and poorly supported specimens of nonviolent defense of justice have been no worse failures than the comparable violent alternatives.[7]

After All

The only alternative which most societies face is an equally programmatic political militarism, which has all the same logical shortcomings. Militarism too places enormous trust in the good intentions and righteousness of its own leaders. Often the nonpacifist accuses the pacifist of being optimistic or unrealistic about sin. But it is the military strategists who make the most sweeping assumptions about the righteousness of their own leaders, their capacity to resist the temptations of power, the quality of their control of their subordinates, and their wisdom.[8] Militarism, just as much as pacifism, misreads the possibility of achieving its goals by the use of its means. Especially it misreads the significance of such labels as freedom or victory when these are identified as goals of immediate action.

Political Pacifism: A Semantic Parenthesis

Within the realm of programmatic pacifism, some distinct variations can usefully be identified. These may be worthy of separate attention. Before I submit a selective catalog of subtypes, it will be helpful for us to give some attention to a question of logic or of conversational procedure underlying the whole debate. In conversations like this, we regularly assume that the definitions we use should properly be borrowed from the nonpacifist mainstream. We tend to assume that the framework of moral thought is the same, that the values to be sought and the facts with which we begin are the same. We suppose that the pacifist differs only in the rejection of certain kinds of means: The question is the same, but the answer is different. The given quantities are the same, but the conclusions to be reached are different.

Creative pacifist political critique hastens to point out that that is not the shape of the question. There is no ground for assuming that the categories of analysis dictated by nonpacifist traditions are adequate. The pacifist does not simply give a minority answer to the majority question. Instead, the pacifist challenges the propriety or utility of the question itself. Two examples must suffice, on coercion and power:

- *Use of Coercion*

It is widely agreed that the use of "the sword" (the ultimate capacity to appeal to the power to coerce) is the sine qua non (i.e., indispensable) definition of the state. If there is no coercive power, there is anarchy. Over against this kind of definition, the political pacifist argues that the police power is not the center but the far edge, the *ultima ratio,* [1] the last resort of any wholesome human community. The health and existence of a community depend upon maintaining the latency of that power.

If coercion is used often, that civilization is less healthy. If people's wills are bent under coercion all the time, that civilization is undergoing tyranny or anarchy. Anarchy is the presence of too much coercive power, not too little. It may be too much to risk the affirmation that there can be ordered societies without any potential recourse to some coercion. Yet beyond that, the practical pacifist can point out that there already have been and are societies where that ultimate recourse practically never needs to be used, or to be legally institutionalized ahead of time.

- *Kinds of Power*

Another widely accepted axiom is that all power is ultimately of the same quality. The differences between the unspoken social pressures of the closed rural community and the outward coercion of urban police are only matters of degree. The difference between the police function and international war are again differences only in degree. It is thus inconsistent, the argument runs, for the pacifist to reject war unless he also rejects police, or to reject killing by police if he is still willing to spank his children.

Now pacifists do vary in their views on spanking children. But practical pacifists all agree that it is simply silly to refuse to recognize the significant qualitative differences which distinguish from one another the several kinds of power. Power, even if it be called "coercive," is of a personal, humane kind as long as the individuals toward whom it is directed are conceived of as persons and their life is protected. The pressures of education, gossip, excommunication, or ostracism are still personal and permit the one against whom they are directed to be restored to the community. The power of office in business, school, or church, or even in nonlethal state functions, can be disciplined by the objectives of those institutions.

This personal quality may perhaps be retained by some exercise of police power. However, it certainly is abandoned in some other kinds of policing and utterly forsaken in war. To argue that "the problem of power is all of one piece" is possible logically, but it gives the common abstraction "power" priority over more significant variables.[2] It is something like saying it is inconsistent for humans to practice contraception if they don't keep their dandelions from breeding, since "the problem of sexual reproduction is all of a piece."

Parenthetically, let us ponder two variations of political pacifism: Responsible Appeasement, and Prudential Calculations:

A. Responsible Appeasement

The word *appeasement* has been almost unspeakable since 1938, when it became the specific label for the acceptance by Britain and France of Hitler's annexation of Czechoslovakia. Yet the root meaning of the term points to what all good government does most of the time, namely, accepting the sacrifice of what would be ideally desirable rather than fight a war about it. This approach is agreed by all to be right in every case where such a sacrifice works and it is possible to avoid hostilities.

The Axiom

It is axiomatic for this view, well documented from experience and still better from contemporary projections, that war, at least modern war, is worse than any other evil which can befall a society. Even when one possesses no immediate plan for achieving all one's desirable purposes, war should still be renounced, for it will not achieve them either. Thus even tragic sacrifices to keep the peace are still preferable to the massive destruction and the hatefulness between peoples which a war causes. Those losses and sacrifices may be great, but they are still less than the losses imposed by war. Willingness to accept them is simply a logical application of calculating lesser evils. Governments always appealed to that same logical process in favor of war when it was less destructive.

A Shortcoming

One flaw is that there is one type of case in which it could be agreed that appeasement is wrong, and then of course it is very wrong, by programmatic political standards. That is the case where the aggressor is not satisfied with the concession made to him, but is thereby only encouraged to become more disorderly and demanding. His ultimate designs for world conquest may be such that it seems nothing will stop him but war. Then politicians responsive to majority opinion may conclude that it only makes things worse to postpone by concessions the confrontation which seems sure to come.

Nevertheless

If we assume, however, that war is the only and always the better alternative to a peaceful concession, that is not (in real experience) the result of rationally and carefully calculating an objective balancing of all the real political possibilities. This assumption, which has given the word *appeasement* a bad sound in the past decades, is imposed on the 1938 Munich agreement from within the history as it is read *after the event* by the winning party.

Appeasement is a fair description to apply only if it is clear in the given case that the aggression lies clearly only on one side and righteousness on the other. It is logical only if it is furthermore established that the particular kind of aggressive intention of the other party is such that it will be increased rather than decreased by having another territory to govern. The more carefully one develops the case for intervention which could be made for 1938, the more clear it becomes that such arguments could apply in few other situations.

But it is more important for us to recognize that only the winning party can ever make this case for war rather than appeasement. The loser in any war would always have been better off to have made peace sooner rather than later, even against an absolutely unjust aggressor. This was demonstrated by the experience of Denmark and the Low Countries in World War II, the Hungarians in 1956, the Czechs in 1968, or the Poles in 1980. Their capacity to resist and later to rise up again was greater precisely because they accepted defeat soon enough to leave their society intact.

After All

If appeasement is to be condemned for failing to sate an aggressor's appetite, armed defense as well would have to be condemned for the far more frequent cases where it has touched off a wider conflagration, or failed seriously to slow down the aggressor. Appeasement can have failed monumentally once and still be preferable, on balance, as a general strategy.

Much hindsight has been used to argue that the Second World War would have been more efficient if it had be-

gun in 1938. Whatever the portion of truth in such a prediction, it avoids asking whether the war, when it was undertaken, did what it was supposed to do. It stopped the
spread of tyranny in Western Europe, but at the cost of
giving the other half of Europe to Stalin. It did not save
Poland for democracy nor save the lives of the Jews. The
more anyone argues a particular case for allied intervention in 1938, the more one must appeal to arguments and
calculations which might in many other cases point in the
other direction. This demonstrates that in such other cases, appeasement, or conciliation and compromise (to use
less tainted terms), would be the responsible thing to do.

The case of Munich should remind us of the special way
in which the U.S. State Department proclaimed the analogy in the late 1960s between Munich and Vietnam and in
the 1990s between Munich and Iraq. That parallel has
served to blur the vision of many. "Never another Munich" has turned out to be a singularly unstatesmanlike
case of misplaced moral absolutism.

Not only must armed defense be tested by its inability
to stop the aggressor; it also appeases. What were Franklin
D. Roosevelt's agreements with Joseph Stalin at Yalta in
1945 if not appeasement on the other side? In return for
the support of a tyrant, the USA did not stop his expansion
and actually conceded to him control over nearly half of
Europe. The allies, in order to win a war, gave away to to-
talitarianism far more territories and populations that
didn't belong to the Allies to give, than Munich gave to
Hitler. To win the Persian Gulf War, USA also made peace
with Syria, thereby doing to Lebanon what Chamberlain
did to Czechoslovakia, and muted the criticism of human
rights abuses in Kuwait, Saudi Arabia, and Palestine. A military alliance is a far less discriminating kind of appeasement than the peacetime concession.

B. The Sobriety of Prudential Calculation

Often the debate about war gets turned in such a way as to make it seem that only the pacifist by commitment to inflexible principle refuses to calculate effectiveness and chances of happy solutions. Yet the pragmatic pacifist can face the challenge of prudential calculation, and can argue cogently and carefully that sobriety about the effects of violence must itself be included in evaluating recourse to violence. The evil of violence corrupts even the relatively righteous intentions of the relatively less-guilty party to a social conflict.

Suppose we grant that in a given conflict members of one party are significantly more righteous than the others, or their cause more just. Even so, the very weapons they resort to, once they have determined that violence is justified, will largely throw away that moral advantage. Good is predicted to result from the war, but that good does not come. Evils not foreseen do actually arise, partly as a result of the very weapons used. Unpredicted evils also arise because members of the more-righteous party are morally diminished as they absolutize their own relative righteousness into an authorization to destroy the adversary.

The historical process generally produces results different from those by which decisions were thought to have been justified. Reinhold Niebuhr described this characteristic as *irony*.[3] Events are impossible to predict with such certainty that moral choices can be made by reasoning back from the predicted outcomes. We should not be surprised at this kind of unpredictability in a universe in which the centers of decision-making are multiple.

Sometimes the historical process is regarded after the model of a machine, where one person pushes the buttons, or even as a nation with a single capital city producing directives. Then to make decisions on the grounds of the simple choice between ultimate outcomes has a certain logic, even though already here it pretends to a utopian degree of omniscience. Yet there are always many other decision-makers in the same causal nexus, each trying to do the same thing, each with a different set of goals, a different set of assumptions about the rules of the whole game and a different set of expectations about how they expect the other partners of the game to play. Therefore, it is a mathematical certainty that we can not be sure that any of the options among which we claim to be choosing can come to pass.

The Axiom

In this position it is axiomatic that the essence of political sobriety is coming to terms with the fact that the problem is people themselves; their reading of the facts and their description of their decisions is warped by their pride. Pragmatism will then be concerned not so much with piling up power and pulling strings as with expecting less and working more modestly. This means calculating more realistically the limits of the attainable, and then letting that sobriety feed back into a powerful skepticism about righteous causes which can justify the use of destructive instruments.

A Shortcoming

Such a modestly prudential pacifism, however, can never solve a problem or prove a point with absolute certainty. It is impossible to demonstrate as an absolute generalization that the evil tools to which the powerful resort will always and completely corrupt those who use them. In a world of relative good and relative evil, it might well be—though it could never be provable—that in a particular case there would be an opposite result: a relatively more wise use of a small, successful war by the relatively more unselfish party might do relatively less harm in the long run than the envisioned prudential alternative.

Nevertheless

Yet this kind of sober, prudential pacifism is the wisest and most honest view of the political scene available. It combines sobriety about the capacity of oneself and one's nation for moral restraint with realism about the ability of coercive instruments to attain valuable goals. In order to state the argument of prudential pacifism, one needs to demonstrate the following in pure logic and not only in statistical probability: it can not be assumed to have been *proved in advance most of the time* that projected results can justify a given destructive behavior in a game with several players. But not only in logic is the proof inconclusive. The record likewise denies everyone's pretensions to determine the course of history by pushing with all one's armed might in what one is sure is the right direction.[4]

After All

The alternative strategy can never prove its projections absolutely either. Weigh the record and the theoretical contemplation of the dynamics of social change. Then the assumption that stronger arms in the hands of good guys are by prudential calculation likely to produce the desired outcomes has a still smaller probability.

5

The Pacifism of Nonviolent Social Change

The power at the disposal of a nonviolent person is always greater than he would have if he were violent. There is no such thing as defeat in nonviolence.
—Mohandas K. Gandhi

Every theology makes some room for the calculation of how most properly to achieve desired ends and prevent undesirable outcomes. In some ethical systems, the calculation of effects is a minor consideration helping only to choose between available permissible ways of applying unchanging principles. In other cases the concept of effectiveness completely takes over the field of ethical deliberation, and there is an explicit avowal of the place of such calculations.

The experience of Gandhi and Martin Luther King has demonstrated that in some kinds of situations, nonviolent methods can effectively bring about social change in the desired direction. Hence, it now is appropriate for both these types of ethical thinkers, those for whom "effectiveness" is the final consideration and those for whom it is considered only instrumentally, to take account of this new information.[1]

Nonviolence as a tool of social change, in particular contexts, has some decided advantages over violence. It can be used by the poor and weak. It gives moral dignity to those who commit themselves to this discipline. That dignity itself makes the action worthwhile even if the effort to change society is not immediately successful. The renunciation of violence robs the oppressor and the adversary of a pretext for resorting to even greater injustice.

This method holds out special promise in areas where other methods have demonstrated their inability to help. In Latin America, for instance, the formula of "revolution" has been tried so often that no one can trust it. It has not generally helped to change the basic social structures. In addition, the polarization of Latin America under the anticommunist surveillance of the United States has contaminated the scene. Even if the internal conditions of a country were such that a revolution of violent character had some chance of success, intervention from the North would make it impossible. This is just one sample of the kind of situation in which nonviolent methods of social change can demonstrably be effective.

The Axiom

Underlying this view is the understanding that it is ultimately in everyone's interest for society to move in the direction of greater justice. The oppressor can be brought to see this by the application of pressures which respect his own humanity and open a way to change without too much loss of face. This view reckons soberly with the reluctance of most people to refrain from evildoing unless they are assured that at least some of their goals can be reached without violence.

Nonviolent social change provides a better path to

those goals. It reckons realistically with the improbability that purely moral considerations (as listed in chapters 1-2, above) will convince many people. Just as politically programmatic pacifism (chapter 4) provides alternative possibilities in international affairs, so this position seeks alternatives to the attitudes and the social structures which make people ready for war.

Shortcomings

Some flaws are inherent within these promises of effectiveness. This method is effective when one can appeal to the conscience of the oppressor, as with Gandhi in India appealing to British self-respect, or the African Americans appealing to the U.S. Constitution. Can it be effective against sadists and brutes? Can it be effective against a regime in which oppression is carried on with a good conscience? Can it maintain its conviction for months or years without any visible success?

The ethical theorist will point out that such a pragmatic nonviolence mixes two kinds of thought.[2] Does it really claim that violence is always wrong, or only that it is usually unwise and ineffective? If the advocate of nonviolence promises success, does this mean that violence would be justified after all if nonviolence were not successful? If on the other hand, it does appeal to a moral absolute or higher law in its rejection of violence, how seriously do we need to take its claim that it will always be effective within the attainable future? By not forsaking the claim to success, it may remain an expression of selfishness, especially if practiced by a whole class, race, or social group.

Especially in its modern form, in which nonviolent techniques have been elaborated quite apart from spiritual disciplines, nonviolence is not in any way specifically Christian. In fact, some have argued that it might be most congenial to the non-Western personality, which is more inured to suffering and less oriented toward either comfort or self-fulfillment, than in Western "Christian" notions of human nature.

Nevertheless

Nonviolent action still remains the only accessible recourse for the oppressed. In some circumstances, it is a most serious option for the morally responsible minority, even those who would have other ways of speaking. Nonviolent action can often be a powerful adjunct to their more traditional processes of opinion formation and political decision.

After All

The honest application of any of the above critical considerations would condemn war even more. War also mixes claims of absolute obligation for which it is better to die, with claims of pragmatic effectiveness which permit acceding to a reasonable peace when one is losing. War as well is demoralizing when it is unsuccessful. War as well is most ineffective when the adversary is irrational or brutal in commitment to violence. Certainly war is not a specifically Christian ethical strategy either. Even if one could claim that the soldier's selfishness is not categorically worse in inward moral quality than the selfishness of the nonviolent crusader, its effect is profoundly different for the victim.

6

The Pacifism of Prophetic Protest

How, they asked, could I be calm about a six-year sentence for pouring blood on draft records? . . . I had thoroughly considered the possible consequences before choosing civil disobedience twice.
—Philip Berrigan, from prison 1968

Some of the positions described above have concentrated on whether, by participating in war, individuals make themselves guilty of sin, before their conscience or before what they understand to be the moral law. More of them have asked whether they place themselves on the wrong side of the course of history, and thus contribute to the wrong chain of causes and effects.

But it is also possible, especially in certain extreme situations, to let one's behavior be dictated not by considerations of right and wrong in either of these accustomed senses, but rather by a concern to communicate. For example: some income tax objectors intend to prevent any dollars that were in their hands from ever getting into the hands of the Pentagon. They are concerned for moral integrity, for having nothing to do with the whole business. Others, however, make no such claim. They admit their inability to keep dollars away from Caesar whose superscription they carry, but still they do not voluntarily pay all their taxes. They are trying to make a point.

Hence, their decision about an action is not weighted only by whether as a deed it is permitted or forbidden by the law of God or by love, but also by what it *says* at a given point. One wants to say something about American society or about colonialism or about the race issue. But the only way you can say this is to do something. This kind of consideration would apply not only to marches and demonstrations and vigils, or to symbolic token actions like tax refusal. It could also apply to a refusal to accept the draft card or a weapon.

The Underlying Axiom

This view holds that thought and action are inseparable, as are word and deed. Human beings are meaning-mongers, whether they speak or not. Every action is a word, and often the unspoken word is louder. Sometimes the unreflective, acted-out thought is more genuine or more logical than the abstraction.

Since this position is motivated by considerations extrinsic to the action itself, to evaluate it as ethics is most difficult. To interpret an act as communication, we would ask whether what it says is true and necessary, and how clearly and surely the message is carried. Usually this will be asked from the perspective of the audience aimed at. Yet sometimes it is to oneself that one must prove something. Sometimes a duty to one's own integrity demands an act of disavowal. This is not necessarily a selfish or self-righteous stance. It may be the only way to state the absoluteness of the moral law. One says one rejects what the moral law rejects, without calculating one's chances of getting away with it or of achieving a change in public policy.

Often the gestures of protest bear a message which is at the same time founded in one of the other types of pacifism of which we have spoken. Then they do not stand alone but are a particular publicity tool. The *parabolic deed* (cf. Jer. 27) can, however, become a type of its own in several ways:

• An absolutist judgment against a particular war may be taken without being subject to the test of whether it would apply in the same way to all other possible wars. The visceral-dramatic dimension can make categorical the present rejection of a particular evil, without rooting it in a philosophically generalized ethic. One can thus make clear how much one cares—at the cost, of course, of not saying clearly why unless words are added.

• War may only be the last straw in one's mounting rejection of a racist, exploitative, dehumanizing system. Without a systematic ethical answer on war itself, one concludes, "This is too much!" and draws the line at war. There the character of the system is preeminently visible.

• War itself is seen as dramatic communication. One asks not only whether killing is wrong, but what war says to one's own people, to the "enemy" population, or to world opinion about political and human values.

• War is arrogance. A nation or a clique of rulers within a given nation will presume to impose their vision of the future on the rest of the world. They claim some moral right or duty by virtue of their own power, success, or philosophy.

• War is idolatry. People make the welfare and the decisions of their own nation an ultimate value to which all else must be sacrificed if necessary.

In these several ways, the necessity of a dramatic, corporally visible *No!* can be perceived in a self-evident way. The protesters may not sense any need to support their rejection either with general lines of reasoning or with alternative courses of action. The rejection of the present evil is valid for its sake, and this must be said by word and deed, whether there is another visible option or not.

Shortcomings

The flaws of this position are serious, intellectually and ethically. We need to bring into play a number of additional variables if we are to be able to evaluate the action of prophetic protesters. It is difficult for any given action to have the same meaning for all involved. A whole group can hardly take a common position without extensive common preparation or regimentation. It is not easy for an action to deliver a confession of faith, a sermon, or an anathema, and not simply be a contribution to the social process.[1]

Even though different conceptions of the objective of a prophetic protest make the choice more complex, yet this kind of declamatory action demands that the protesters have a powerful sense of moral certainty. Self-righteous claims to a unique prophetic authority are almost necessarily implicit when one takes such a stance. Yet such arrogance may also be a kind of violence toward those receiving the communication. Thus we need to ask to what extent the prophetic communication is understood as intended by the protesters. Does the message get through?

Nevertheless

The perception of the moral meaningfulness of deeds with which this position begins is still correct. The conformity of the masses to whatever the rulers are doing is a powerful word of support for present policies. Vocal dissent is of little weight if it is not linked with dissenting action. The negative vote which goes no further than voting is one kind of dissenting voice. The refusal to cooperate with the majority decision is a voice of another magnitude. Especially in our age of verbal overload, the ears and the brain sift out much that they hear and the memory drops most of what was read. So the amplifier which the acted word becomes is the only way for some messages to be heard.

After All

It is usually, often to an even greater degree, characteristic of war that it purposes to *say* something, and that concern for that meaning complicates its moral evaluation. Youths who enlist are often trying to say something to themselves or their parents about their growing up. Bearing arms is a demonstration of strength or dependability.

Nationally, the recourse to war or the insistence on staying in a war may be motivated not by the political ends to be sought in themselves, by the repulsion of specific aggression, or the possibility of setting up a peaceful order. Instead, in USA, the Vietnam case dramatically illustrated other motivations during a decade and the Persian Gulf even more dramatically for six months. We desire to communicate to others that we will not be pushed around, that we are people who keep our promises, or that communist aggression does not pay anywhere. Our rulers have spoken overtly about this "message" dimension, claiming thereby to justify belligerence against Nicaragua, Grenada, Panama, and especially Iraq.

What we communicate by killing is even less clear, and it is even harder to make a moral case for that message. It differs from the nonviolent types of protest in that the enemy, the victim, can receive our message that we want him to drop dead, but then no longer has a chance to respond or change. To the extent to which the warlike action is successful, it can communicate only to another *public.* We crush Vietnam or Iraq for the sake of what must be proved to the Chinese or the Russians or the Burmese or ourselves about the American character. We want a "shot heard round the world." On the other hand, nonviolent demonstration seeks to communicate an affirmation of human dignity to the ones to whom it is addressed, and whom it inconveniences.

7

The Pacifism of Proclamation

As [the church] encountered this call historically, not only in Jesus' words, but in his death and resurrection, so also the church can make this message effectual only by passing it along in her deeds of authentic witness.
—Hans-Werner Bartsch

All of the positions sketched above have rooted their ethical thought in some conception of righteousness. Ethics is seen as an expression of concern for the integrity of persons in their decisions. The propriety of an act is seen as measured against the demands of the law, or the rightness of an act is seen in its social effects.

In Christian ethics we have largely concentrated on these dimensions for centuries. In so doing, we have missed another major dimension of Christian concern, one especially vital in the New Testament and increasingly seen as central in the essence of the Protestant Reformation and the missionary vision of the church.

This missing element is the understanding of the total Christian life as an aspect of the proclamation of the kingdom of God. Jesus, like his predecessor John, certainly understood his very being and not only his words as a living sermon. Jesus' words were proclamation, but so were his healings and exorcisms; so was his very presence.

This centering of ethical concern into proclamation constitutes the unfinished business of the Protestant Reformation. The Reformation reoriented the reading of the Bible and the celebration of the sacraments around the concept of proclamation. Specifically, the message to proclaim was unconditional forgiveness, or "justification by faith." This perspective increasingly penetrated dogma and missionary thought. But theologians never succeeded to the same extent in thinking of Christian *behavior* as proclamatory or kerygmatic.

If ethics can be illuminated from the kingdom message, it will break the bounds of the other views. An ethic of law, of effects, or of personal integrity is an ethic which enables people to be righteous. One can plan one's behavior and interpret God's demands in such a way that the right action is feasible. But so to tailor one's understanding of God's demands that one is sure to be able to meet them is already self-righteousness.

The proclamation that the kingdom of God is at hand gives us a new criterion of possibility. We henceforth cease to calculate what is normally, humanly feasible. We no longer resign ourselves to less than the best.

The proclamation of the kingdom is at the same time a new criterion of righteousness. That action is good which communicates to my neighbors the coming of the kingdom for them. Beyond this, proclamation is a new criterion of the center of Christian truth: the coming of the kingdom means that God has now made me really to be the servant of my neighbor.

Ethics in the New Testament reflects this proclamatory mood in the way it mixes prediction and promise in its commands. It is impossible to distinguish *you are* from *you shall* and *you ought*. Christian obedience is not derived from calculating how to meet requirements in order to receive rewards. Instead, the believer's life works out obedience in a new divinely decreed context.[1]

Now, in the case of war, I am asked to deal with the enemy people who are the neighbor I am to love. My action must be such as to communicate or proclaim to them the nature of God's love for them. It might be possible to argue that this could be done with a certain kind of force, moral or social or even physical, but certainly it cannot be said by threatening or taking their life.

The Axiom

Underlying this approach is the Protestant one that the proclamation of the Word of God is the true motor of history and the locus of its meaning. It is not the business of Christian obedience to protect or improve upon this Word, to filter it, to support it, or to bend it to fit cases and possibilities. We are simply to speak it and to live from faith in its finality, as Hans-Werner Bartsch writes:

> The Sermon on the Plain proclaims salvation unconditionally, without respect for human possibility. Christians experienced this proclamation historically in the encounter with the risen Lord, in that through this encounter the rescuing of the lost by God's intervention was attested. Now the church passes on this same assurance in her own preaching. But just as this affirmation historically came to the church not only in the word of Jesus but in his death and resurrection, so she can pass on this proclamation with historic effectiveness only by behavior which has the character of a witness.
>
> The attesting of salvation is not a supplemental assignment, added as a second requirement to that of the acceptance of salvation. The acceptance of salvation

itself only occurs in the act of the testimony which passes it on. Therefore, the church, to the extent to which she is true to the church of Jesus Christ, which names Jesus as Lord, is directed to the neighbor. The social significance of the church is given in her commission to witness, because this commission necessarily includes behavior toward the neighbor.[2]

Shortcomings

This kind of position has serious weaknesses, especially when we seek to commend it to non-Christians or Christians of quite other traditions. It is most clearly and convincingly stated in the writings of a few Lutheran theologians and is most at home in the Lutheran context.[3] European Protestant thought has been compelled by Karl Barth to let theology as a "science" (i.e., an intellectual discipline with its own rules and its own intrinsic dignity) define its own terms and refuse to be judged by the assumptions of any other intellectual approach. It has been conditioned as well by the heritage of Rudolf Bultmann, who in an equally unaccountable way locates the meaning of reality in an inexplicable self-awareness of one's identity.

Thus continental neo-Protestant thought is quite able to conceive of normative Christian proclamation as setting its own terms. It makes *sui generis* (qualitatively unique) demands which need not be tested and in fact cannot be tested by the standards of any other stance. This is not proud solipsism; it is an extremely humble position. It denies to the theologian as intellectual the right to call God to account for the strangeness of his ways of speaking. Thus it refuses to the thinker the license to improve and adapt God's message.

Yet problems do arise in conversation with other Christian traditions, and especially in conversation with the world and with other disciplines. When we insist upon stating Christian proclamation in the right and not the wrong terms and demand that we think in a new mode of thought because the gospel demands it, others may perceive that as provincial or as proud.

A further shortcoming of this position appears as it affirms the unconditional possibility of proclaiming love to the neighbor. It makes this statement without reference to cases and details, thus providing no clear guidance for the case-by-case decisions which we do have to keep on making. Shall a proclamatory pacifism always seek neutrality in every political conflict, or can it take sides nonviolently? Can it even accept that one kind of violence is less evil than another?

One may state that it is precisely the enemy who is the neighbor I am to love, and that the coming of the kingdom of God makes all things new. Yet that does not immediately answer those questions. Is this Word then not an abstraction? We may set up as an ethical guide the statement, "My action must proclaim God's unmerited love for the godless." Yet might that commitment not after all fail to communicate, to be Word?

Nevertheless

Yet this is the Protestant axiom. It is true that Jesus' deeds, especially his dealings with sickness and with foreigners, and with hunger and with violence, have a word dimension. It is correct that freeing ethics from the link to justification would be a consistent extension of Luther's program of freeing justification from works.

After All

As we have just seen in a wider context, war also proclaims an understanding of God and how he deals with sinners. War always does communicate a message about whether we think the people we are dealing with are objects of God's love or not. This is so especially when we say that a war is being prepared for peace or freedom, carried on in the name of peace or freedom, or to teach the world a lesson. In the modern world, every war proclaims something about human character and usually also something about race and wealth.

Most Christians and most military agencies have not built and do not build a clear casuistic fence to identify the limits of their use of violence. As long as this is true, all militarism is likewise running away from serious case-by-case discipline, and taking refuge in unaccountable abstract proclamations of virtue.

Parenthesis: Program and Practicality

The varieties dealt with thus far have all taken seriously in one way or another the challenge of program. They are ready to write a recipe for society, though they vary in the ways in which they found their opposition to war and motivate it. Yet there is a significant variation along another scale to which we have not yet paid attention: how closely does practice need to follow the prescription? For some, the mere possession of an alternative vision includes an immediate obligation to lobby or propagandize for that policy. For others, this does not necessarily follow at all. Such variations would apply within most of the types of thought identified above. We pause here for a sketchy kind of subcatalog.

A. How Practical Must We Be?

1. There are those for whom a practical alternative must, by definition, be one which can *win acceptance* and actually be applied. The advocacy of the alternative is then not complete until, through all the channels of due process, the rudder of the state can be turned. In that case,

practical means not only that the policy, if applied, would resolve the international problems. It means also that the policy must be one which can win acceptance by the people, or at least by the people in power.[1]

2. Others may agree to reckon seriously with the same obligation of efficacy. Yet they may recognize that the political system is so corrupted by hidden interests and lines of power that it will never do the right thing of its own accord. There is, however, the extreme recourse of *civil disobedience,* conceived as an emergency appeal from due process to the consciences of the public or those in office. They hope suffering and shock will reach where letters to journals and statesmen cannot. The objectors, though disobedient, remain within the limits of submission and accept their punishment.

3. Civil disobedience of *the test case* lies somewhere between these first two forms. It may be seen either as a most extreme form of due process or as a most modest form of civil disobedience. Which it will be, will be decided not by the dissenter but by the system. Here one appeals not to the conscience of others but rather to another branch of government. One may appeal to the courts against the excesses of the executive or the impotence of the legislature. If sustained by the courts, the test case has been a successful experience of due process. If not sustained, then one is in the posture of civil disobedience, but the claim that the law one broke was unjust has been somewhat weakened by the failed effort to prove one's innocence.[2]

4. Still more critical of "the system" is the stance that has been called (in a shift of the meaning of the adjective) *uncivil disobedience.* A minority no longer believes that it is possible to appeal to the consciences of others. Yet they can force their will on the majority, or obtain negotiating leverage, if they are willing to jeopardize property, or to block the normal functioning of civil administration, the

economy, urban transportation, or the university. They may run the risk of violence, though not intending to kill. They uphold the claim to programmatic effectiveness, but the goal set can be achieved only coercively, by forcing someone to back down. If they do not succeed, the effect is generally to harden the adversary's resolve. Both the advocates of racial justice and the critics of the Vietnam War began acting in this less "civil" spirit in the U.S. around 1967.

B. How Real Is the Option?

The spectrum drawn above (in order of increasing alienation) progresses in the degree of opposition to the authorities. It retains the claim that one's action is justified by one's chances of bringing about the results sought. There is, however, a different line along which it is possible to vary in the way one interrelates feasibility and responsibility.

1. The claim to present a *practical alternative* may be quite clear and concrete, as it often is with Quaker study documents.[3] The path suggested is one which could really be taken, starting from here, if one wished.

2. On the other hand, one can retain the claim that a given international conflict *could have been resolved*, but not concede that one's right to uphold this claim is tested by whether one can bring rulers or population to practice it. "You could have done otherwise" may clothe a word of prophetic condemnation. That needs to be proclaimed as a denunciation of idolatry in the full awareness that warring parties will not repent, or that it is too late for repentance to save them.

"You need not be the slaves of the vicious circle of violence" may be a gospel invitation which only a few will hear even as the unheeding masses rush on. "You will be sorry you chose this path" may be a warning which later will enable some to find the grace of repentance. In any of these contexts, the practicable yet unpractical programmatic option finds its relevance not as a real path we may take tomorrow, but as a way to clothe the call to reconciliation in the success-centered mythic language of our time.

3. In still another way one can contemplate practical options without needing to be able to implement them. They may be *pedagogical paradigms*, ways of testing one's thought patterns, techniques to clarify logical options. One may look at pragmatic options in order to undercut the nonpacifist's claim that only war is realistic and the pacifist is utopian. Or one may entertain options as a way of entering conversation with those whose habits of thought are limited to short-range ends-means calculations, even while one's own position is not limited to or judged by such criteria.[4] "War is not a usable instrument; there would be other ways" protects pacifists against the accusation that they do not care or do not deal with reality. Yet that statement does not commit them to deliver a nonviolent solution which actually can win acceptance.

The strategic difference between these positions has been publicly debated in recent years, in close linkage to the issues of Vietnam and race, nuclear arms and liberation. As a result, many observers regard these complexities as a peculiar burden of the concerns of peace and racial justice. For some, the resulting debates among pacifist and race-relations agencies may seem even to discredit the pacifist concern. This is a wrong reading of the facts.

These variations are visible around the peace issue because it is an important issue. But the same set of problems in instrumentation would have to be faced if we were concerned about moral dimensions of contraception, prohibition, the single tax for Keynesian economic controls, urban transportation, or guaranteed income. The same variations in degrees of real practicality apply just as well in the military realm. They plague the strategy thought of the white citizens' councils and survivalists, as much as they do that of the civil rights movements. There is thus no weight to the notion that they weigh particularly against nonviolent views or in favor of violent ones.

8

The Pacifism of Utopian Purism

There is no way to peace: peace is the way.
—Abraham J. Muste[1]

Since the 1960s there is a much greater awareness and recognition than earlier that the New Testament style of discourse, imitated in the recent "hyperbolic" or "utopian" language of the counterculture, is not culturally or morally irrelevant. It can stand over against pragmatism as a credible alternate vision of the relationship between the good and the real. In addition, it exposes the contradiction in means and ends of those who cast aside the good in order to accomplish it.[2]

A society which hates its enemies and, although it says killing is wrong, punishes killers by killing them—thereby telling them that they were right—is so twisted that it is unworthy of defense. We cannot get from here to the Holy City by compromise or by calculated risks, but only by a leap of faith.

Some people claim to be relevant and able to measure out their creativity and their courage in small doses, so as not to be crucified. But they have not proved that their compromise increased their efficacy. A purely utopian ethic asks to be evaluated by its consistency, not by its results. It is, as far as we know, still just as efficient as one which seeks efficiency as a goal. Did not Jesus say that it was when we forsake all for the kingdom that everything else will be added to us? Did he not say as well by implication that those who seek first the other things will miss both the "other things" and the kingdom?

There is then no real need for us to prop up our rejection of war by considerations of how that rejection will itself improve the world. Nor need we calculate how our rejection of war can be more responsible or acceptable if it is less consistent.

This position can be called a "purism"—if that be thought of as a descriptive and not a pejorative term—not because it lays claim to the purity of guiltlessness or perfect achievement, but because it demands and offers a qualitative newness of relationships from which every justification given for hostility has been banned. It is the demand of the categorical imperative: Let my behavior be governed by the criterion that I must do only that which, if everyone did it, would bring a new order.

The Axiom

Underlying this position is the belief that we all are made for a city of love and that we cannot enter it through the gates of concession and compromise. We will have no rest until that city is realized. One gets there not by compromising with the present but by confessing a faith which makes the future real in symbolic ways today.

Shortcomings

It is no argument against this position to say that it does not accept the criterion of responsibility. The utopian pacifist can argue in return that the criterion of responsibility itself becomes a self-justifying and ultimately self-defeating idolatry. This is not a position which will be greatly effective in winning respect of the typical Western pragmatist committed to calculating yield per unit of input. Yet is not that way of calculating already part of the sickness from which we are seeking to help modern people leap free?

One disadvantage of this position is that, to those whom it challenges, it seems to be of no assistance. It looks like a new form of the monastic retreat, living parasitically on the very system which it rejects. If the ideal society stands only in a purely negative relationship to the society in which we live, where then do you get the ideal by which you judge? Which of the possible ideals from which one might judge the present is right, and how do you know that? Do you not confirm the present system in its fallen implacability just as much by refusing to talk with it as by working with it?

The purist position can explain its refusals but not its continuities. The spirit of revolution cannot be institutionalized; if the "New Left" of the sixties is in the nineties it is no longer new. The question raised by this position is not so much a flaw in its pacifism, its judgment on the evil powers of society, as in its wider vision of human nature, its trust in the goodness of the moral self of the purist.

Nevertheless

Utopias and apocalypses may still be the most powerfully responsible instruments of change. A patient depth reading of history points in this direction. If, as Jesus says, pragmatic utilitarianism is self-defeating because self-fulfillment is found only in self-forgetfulness,[3] might there not be an analogy to this on the social-moral level? Might it not be that the most right action is the one most forgetful of its ramifications? That God's sovereignty might enter ethics at the point of denying one's accountability to the prudential calculations of those of little faith?

After All

This utopian pacifism trusts less to an irrational leap of faith than does the rhetoric which tells us that by forcibly making refugees, we are defending self-determination; or that by supporting a puppet government, we are enabling democracy to grow. There is no more utopian institution than an idealistic war. The Atlantic Charter or the Wilsonian fourteen points are utopian documents, no more responsibly meshed with the historical realities than is the vision of the New Jerusalem in Revelation 20. War is utopian both in the promises it makes for the future and in the black-and-white way of thinking about the enemy, which it assumes.

The utopian character of war has been demonstrated repeatedly in the past century in the outworkings of the assumption that after we defeat the one bad nation, the forces of good can go home. We were told in the USA that the invasion of Panama would endow that country with freedom and prosperity. The Persian Gulf War was supposed to inaugurate a "New World Order."

The warmaker is utopian in believing that there will ever be a world in which world moral leadership can be exerted by a nation whose overseas presence is predominantly commercial and military. It is utopian in continuing to believe, or at least to say that it believes, that one can win a war without committing atrocities. It is utopian in believing that the only obstacle to peaceful settlement is the inexplicable obstinacy of the other side.

In all these dimensions (speaking now for the United States civilization), it is the purist vision which seems to be guiding United States policies overseas. That purism is the product of the morality of the Western novel or film, with the easily (ethnically) identified good guys and bad guys, and the unlimited justification of violence in the hands of the good.

9

The Pacifism of the Virtuous Minority

The regenerated do not go to war nor engage in strife. Spears and swords of iron we leave to those, who, alas, consider human blood and swine's blood of well-nigh equal value.
—Menno Simons, 1539.

The church appreciates and prays for the government. It also gives to the government a clear testimony as its own convictions on war, but there is no attempt to control the government, and no demand that it follow a given course with respect to specific points of foreign policy. Its only demands are those which the New Testament directs to Christians themselves as regenerated members of the kingdom of God.
—Guy F. Hershberger, *War, Peace, and Nonresistance*

Ever since Constantine, it is a normal reflex in everyone's ethical thought to assume that, when we ask about right behavior, we are seeking a standard to apply consistently to all people. It is always thought to be a fair test to ask "What if everybody did this? Can you ask this of everyone?"[1] This line of thought generally supports the legitimation of war, because of the self-evident need to save society and because of the unreadiness of many persons to live sacrificially.

We can plausibly doubt that the sacrifices demanded by war are ultimately so much easier to make than those demanded by nonviolent love. We can doubt that war does actually save society. Those arguments, however, are not our present concern.

Instead, on simply logical grounds, we call into doubt this axiom that the same ethics are for everybody. The same question is raised in different forms from within several religious traditions. Within Roman Catholicism there is the ancient tradition of the "evangelical counsels." These guidelines hold up before people the call to a level of morality distinct from that of merely keeping the law. Poverty and loving one's enemies are things that not everyone has to do, but it would be fine if some did. All are invited to live on this level, but not all are expected or required so to live. The members of a religious order are more likely expected actually to be able to live on the level of these counsels, which are not enforced by law and not expected of everyone.

Within the pietist and Wesleyan traditions there is the somewhat similar concept of "Christian perfection." This again is a level of moral being, and of performance derived from that level of being, which is not assumed to be given to or demanded of all people. Life on this level is not a matter of demand but a very special gift.

Protestantism in general has not explicitly developed this kind of vision of a minority morality. It runs counter to some of the major emphases of the mainstream Reformation. In practice, however, most Protestants do expect of their pastor and of the missionary a higher level of wholesomeness and unselfishness than they expect of themselves. This is quite distinguishable from the kind of life which they assume the church has a right to ask of the rest of them.

In a different form, the ethic of the free church or believers church tradition within Protestantism[2] is likewise not an ethic for everyone. Discipleship after the pattern of the humanity of Jesus may well be the calling of all, be they Christian or not, aware of their calling or not. But that calling can only become a concrete expectation in the life of the individual and in the practice of the church if members have committed themselves to a discipline in response to that call.

The *believers church,* constituted of adult members who have joined the community by their own choice, holds that all Christians must be committed to full discipleship. But it is not meaningful to expect the same quality of life from others who have not made that commitment, and therefore improper to seek to enforce it for others. Non-Christians cannot equally draw upon the resources of forgiveness and regeneration, the guidance of the Spirit, and the counsel of fellow believers. Christianity is for everybody; but Christian ethics is a normal, natural expectation for Christians.[3]

This type of minority morality had already made it clear in the Middle Ages that killing must be rejected for persons who live on the level of the gospel. In Catholic canon law, it still applies to the cleric and the member of a religious order, and it is recognized in the laws of some states. This probably explains the cultural and emotional rootage of *conscientious objector* privileges in Western legal systems, even though these have then come to be extended to persons who understand their position in other terms.

The Axiom

Underlying this view is the understanding that morality finds its context in a freely covenanted response to the call of God. In this joyful fellowship, life is freed from concern both for personal merit and for demonstrable results. The good is not what promises to move the world in the right direction. The good is experienced in responding to the nature of God as he has graciously manifested himself, and in participating already in the nature of that toward which the world must move.

The first step is to free morality from the bind of needing to meet the test of applicability to all. Then we are for the first time able to look at the good action as a question distinct from judgmental casuistry. We observe that deed which has about it the quality of conformity to the goodness of God. This is what is meant by our title's reference to the virtuous minority.[4]

Only if we recognize that ethics is not generalizable are we free to use in a wholesome way the concept of virtue, of good that is intrinsic in certain kinds of action or character. This pattern of thought is demanded by biblical language with its catalogs of virtues and vices. It is strongly supported, not only by the tradition of monastic self-discipline, but also by the stoic naturalism of the modern person's self-cultivation. Violence is a vice to be avoided. Nonviolence or meekness is a virtue and to be cultivated.

Shortcomings

There are flaws in this type of minority pacifism. Once its adherents have withdrawn from the majority, they may acquiesce in the compromises made by the majority in their own interest, and thereby undermine their claim to be heard as critics. The "monastic" few may accept minority status, feel pride in it, and feel set apart by it, rather than regarding it as living out a call addressed to all people. This temptation is built-in, especially if one develops a theory of two moral levels,[5] an intentional double standard for clergy and laypersons, or for church and world.

A quite analogous temptation besets the sectarian Protestant form of minority morality. The minority can easily become ecumenically irresponsible, unconcerned for the needs or concerns or commitments of other Christians. Sometimes the search for a virtue is not anchored pragmatically and becomes obscurantist, or is self-centered and thereby self-righteous. One may seek to save one's own soul by turning the back to others. Thus one may be too easily reconciled to the inability of the minority to do any good in a wider world.

One normal implication of this minority stance is to approve by implication, for most people, the very position one rejects for oneself. The Catholic understanding of the monastic morality has no trouble with this. Those in this tradition do not identify the freely chosen Rule with everyone's moral obligation. They tell Christians in the Historic Peace Churches to accept such minority status and be accepted in it. Thus the minority stance can be a special gadfly performance to keep the rest of society from being at peace with its compromises.

This understanding of a vocational role for the peace churches has been fostered by the relativistic or pluralistic mood of modern denominationalism. The question of objective right and wrong is relativized by the acceptance of a great variety of traditions, each having its own claims to truth arising out of its own history. Each may be recognized as having a portion of the truth, on condition that none impose their view on another.

What in denominational pluralism arises out of democratic self-restraint, becomes in some contemporary Protestant theologies a committed relativism. This indefiniteness is founded in a view of truth as itself having no firm landmarks, but consisting in the interplay of several positions. Various stances may be recognized as "valid" or "authentic" or "adequate," but none specifically as *true*. In this spirit many nonpacifists since the 1930s have been willing to concede to the pacifists a prophetic or vocational role.[6] Nonpacifists grant this recognition on condition that in turn the pacifists accept always being voted down by those who have to do the real (violent) work in the world.

Ultimately, such an acceptance of minority status as defined on majority terms is morally unsatisfactory. It concedes to the majority that for the majority the position of compromise is justified. It agrees that a position faithful to the gospel cannot be practiced within real life. It further courts the danger of complacency or self-righteousness for the persons or group taking the "set-apart" position which is acknowledged to be morally superior. At the same time they are released, under the mantle of mutual tolerance, from the discipline of seeking to commend their position effectively to others.[7]

Peace church members who accept the "vocational" label tend to use it as a cover for failing to be clear on their own convictions and the relevance of those convictions to their fellow believers and the world. They affirm Jesus as their own guide but not as Lord over the cosmos. Yet they still take credit for a consistent stance.

Nevertheless

Yet the morality of the New Testament is a minority morality, and the same will be the case wherever the Christian church lives in genuine missionary nonconformity. The pacifism of the minority avoids the puritan legalism which would seek to impose upon all persons a level of performance for which they do not have the spiritual or educational resources. It also avoids the latitudinarian legalism which spends its efforts planning pretexts for permitting almost anything because someone is going to have to do it anyway.

Only in the minds of critics has the nonconformist minority renounced social effectiveness. At least in certain times and places and ways, this stance is the presupposition of any meaningful communication. One excellent modern sample of this is Dorothy Day, the spirit at the heart of the Catholic Worker movement.[8] For two generations she was at the center of a movement of charity and social nonconformity possessing almost no settled constituency and no legal status. Yet the bishops at Vatican II listened to her, simply because of the symbolic quality and integrity of her commitment.

After All

War likewise has its own minority ethic, that of the SS or the Green Beret. Special military units, paratroopers, marines, and commandos of various kinds, Western movie and espionage heroes—these have always been especially honored and publicly rewarded for practicing a morality which would not be tolerated within an orderly society. Certainly the spiritual danger of self-congratulation is no less in this case.

On the international scale, the vision of an elite calling has long been used as a justification of war. That model has been applied just as proudly, and far more destructively, than the pacifists' sense of privilege has ever been applied to their abstention from war. The Knights Templar and the Order of Malta, the white man's burden and the saving of Asia from communism—these all have justified war under the label of a unique and righteous calling which other persons or nations do not have.

10

The Pacifism of the Categorical Imperative

The kingdoms of this world may become the kingdom of the Lord and of his Christ.
—H. J. Cadbury

It seems practically self-evident to the average Western mind that any ethical commitment can be most usefully tested by the question: "What happens if everybody does it?" In the heritage of Christendom, it used to be realistic to assume, when speaking about right and wrong, that everyone would be listening, and in fact would have to obey. It was assumed that theologians could do the moral thinking for the whole of Western Christian civilization, for whom the Christian church was recognized as the authoritative moral teacher. This called for every moral decision to be evaluated by *two tests*, which usually coincide in their effect but may be distinguished in their logic:

- What will happen if it becomes public policy? What if the king or the president would do this?
- What would happen if everybody did it?

We have referred earlier to the impact of this kind of assumption when it is linked with further predefinitions of the goals which must be met by a public policy. People wonder how much unselfishness can be expected of persons in large numbers or in large groups. Such logic leads to one of the most self-evident kinds of justification not only for violence but also for class and national egoism. For this reason we pointed out above (chapter 9) that the assumptions of this Christendom logic of generalizability are by no means self-evident. It might be more appropriate to say that Christian ethics should seek to be able to meet the test of another set of questions:

- What will happen if *not* everyone does it?
- What will happen if what Christians do is *not* public policy?
- What would be intrinsically "right" to do if we had no occasion to calculate "what will happen"?

Although I am pointing to the limits of the criterion of generalizability in moral logic, this does not mean that I grant the claimed universality (and consequent legitimacy) of group selfishness. Nor should it be granted as proved that this "Christendom" mode of thought always works in favor of violent positions. Immanuel Kant stated what he called "the categorical imperative": "Act in the way you wish everyone would." He meant this dictum to function not as a screen to filter out every idealism on the ground that not everyone is likely to be willing to share it, but rather as a prod to setting higher goals.

The Unspoken Axiom

Behind this approach is the assumption that one of the safest ways I can seek to stand in judgment upon my own propensities to selfishness is a mental act of generalization. In that act I posit others, or all others, as the moral agent. I can ask how things would look if everyone else did what I contemplate doing.

By "everyone" we *might* mean not "the majority of people as they are now," but rather "our vision for the way the world should become." If so, then we can understand much of the liberal and utopian pacifism of the 1930s in its most authentic light. Test how you want to behave by whether you would want to live in a world where everybody would act as you do. Would you want a world where every prince and every parliament reserves the right of wrathful redress? If not, then you must make the renunciation of coercion and retaliation the law of your own community.

Suppose everyone in the U.S. were a conscientious objector. Then, true enough, the American capacity to influence governments around the world would be much less if they only respect a big stick. But so would the American crime rate be less. We would at least be sure that American cities would never be destroyed by an atomic exchange nor by an invading army. American integrity might then produce more long-term good effect in the international scene. The funds and personnel available for influencing the world in peaceful ways and for healing our society would be increased by more than half the present federal budget. The hypothetical test is not a very probable one, but it still makes a clear point.

Shortcomings

This kind of reasoning is full of logical loopholes. As self-evident as it seems at first, it is not a fully helpful kind of proof. We can rather easily dramatize the limited usefulness of putting questions this way by reminding ourselves that a society populated completely by conscientious objectors would have little crime, no military expenditures, and large resources available for social welfare causes. To say that I would want to live in a world where everyone would treat me the way I would want to be treated may be a sign of psychological immaturity. It certainly has no direct relation to any questions we really ask or have any occasion to solve in concrete ethical decisions.

Nevertheless

Yet it would be irresponsible for us not to take some cognizance of the fact that in the Western world, Christian moral thought does impinge on a large element of society. It reaches well beyond the committed members of disciplined Christian communities. When clearly spoken, Christian appeals for international aid, civil rights legislation, extension of the right of education, or protection of the rights of minorities have had a public effect. "Would you want to be in a world where everyone does it?" may be considered a reformulation of the golden rule[1] onto the social scale.

Its most logical implication is to remind us to ask critically what the world would be like if every nation felt called to police half of the world. Or what a society would come to be like if everyone were a soldier. Especially the pacifist implications become clear if one recognizes the illogic of limiting generalizability to one nation. Suppose everyone in this country were a conscientious objector. Then by the same hypothetically miraculous conversion, it would be just as realistic to posit that at least most people in most other countries would also be considerably more peaceable than they are today. Therefore, they would constitute much less of a threat.

After All

It is still the traditionally promilitary argument which uses this appeal most readily. The question to a pacifist, "What if everybody did it?" is second in frequency only to

"What if a burglar . . .?"[2] These objections seem to be most self-evidently convincing to those who have not thought much about the arguments. The nonpacifist mind can hardly tolerate any challenge to making the nation as a whole or the ruler the proper agent of ethical decision. Then it ought to be a fair argument to point out that the "categorical" reasoning really works the other way if you recognize the rest of humanity: What if other nations acted like ours?

11

The Pacifism of Absolute Conscience

"I cannot serve as a soldier," said Maximilianus. "I cannot do evil; I am a Christian."

Dion told him: "In the retinue of our lords . . . there are Christian soldiers and they serve."

Maximilianus replied, "They are responsible for their own doings."

Maximilianus was sentenced to death and the sentence was immediately carried out.

—The story of a noble martyr, 295

It is undeniably a part of human personality, or at least of the personality of certain persons, that they are possessed by an undeniable, irrefutable, immediate conviction of right and wrong. This "conscience" will be nourished and given content by experience and education. Yet in the immediacy of its claims upon the person, and in its choice of when and how deeply the person will be concerned about certain issues, it cannot be fully explained by educational considerations.

This conscience expresses itself by using all kinds of arguments, and may in the course of time in turn be modified by all kinds of arguments. But at the moment of immediate certainty, its claim for obedience is not debatable, nor can it be tested by any criterion outside itself. The immediate conviction of conscience short-circuits the logical linkage between general moral considerations and particular conclusions.

The Axiom

Underlying current American usage is the assumption that a person's conscience will tell oneself "yes" or "no" in ways the individual can neither doubt nor explain. It is this immediate and immeasurable absolute which government respects when it recognizes conscientious objection. As recent USA experience demonstrates, government would rather not have conscientious objectors be too articulate about their position or too able to make selective application to different kinds of situations. Indeed, if it is not an immediate and irrational position, it does not qualify for some people's understanding as conscience. If an objector's position is too rational and selective, it is rejected as "not conscientious but philosophical."

Thus most of the traditional ethical systems teach that it is the duty of individuals to obey the dictates of conscience even if wrongly informed. The integrity of the person is the presupposition of all morality. Therefore, in the short run and in the presence of inadequate information, it is better to preserve that integrity by obeying a wrongly informed conscience than to wound one's conscience by doing the objectively right thing while thinking it wrong.

Shortcomings

This position has serious limits. It is subject to no theological or moral criteria outside itself. The autonomous conscience is therefore just as likely to be idolatrous as obedient. Persons claiming only grounds of conscience escape other kinds of moral accountability and community. They may be utterly sincere and utterly wrong. They can be doing the right and somehow not feel right about it.

Nevertheless

Yet in a society (such as the Christian church), not everyone can or should be a professional ethicist constantly able to reinspect every link on the chain between general principles and concrete choices. Hence, the shortcut represented by conscience is indispensable. If we are to go on with the work, there must be certainties not constantly reexamined. Their claim on one's allegiance must be more than rational, else one would spend all energies negotiating about their fringes and loopholes.

One may consider conscience in some inexplicable sense the voice of God, or a distillate of the social memory of the individual. Either way, such a logical shortcut honors and fosters the individual's moral integrity by giving each one a clear way to practice saying an unambiguous "I cannot do otherwise."[1] That is far more wholesome both socially and psychologically than either a hardened, unquestioning conscience or an artificially maintained, permanently anguished openness.

After All

The alternative seems to be an equally irrational and irresponsible blind acceptance of the behavior patterns or the legal demands of the surrounding society. To do conscientiously whatever one is told by the state to do is morally just as unaccountable before God as promising to obey the inexplicable dictates of one's own insight.

12

The Pacifism of Redemptive Personalism

Governments rather depend upon men than men upon governments. Let men be good, and government cannot be bad. If it be ill, they will cure it. But if men be bad, let the government be ever so good, they will endeavor to warp and spoil it to their tune.
—William Penn, 1684

Human beings are at the root of all evil. Therefore, people must change if the evil of the world is to be changed. They cannot be changed by reliance on the same kind of evil which already is the mark of their misery. Violence perpetuates evil by continuing the chain of evil causes and effects, condemning humanity to the vicious circle of continuing hate and destruction. No amount of greater power or of greater modesty in using evil against evil will get at the root of the problem.

The "personalism" of which we speak here is "redemptive": it makes a new start at its own expense. The redemptive personalist will refuse to cooperate in evil, will break the chain of evil causes and effects, and will take the resultant suffering upon oneself. This is an expression of respect for the person of the adversary. Nonviolence in this form is an appeal to the conscience of the person with whom one deals.[1] The readiness to suffer arises out of the recognition of the dimensions of evil and the impossibility of conquering it without suffering its evil effects.

This position can fittingly be taken by Christians, but it may meaningfully be taken by others as well.[2] Its most substantial and theologically rooted Christian form is the Quaker understanding of "speaking to that of God in every man."[3]

Without denying the reality of institutional structures and responsibility, this personalism discerns at the center of most institutions a man or a team or a clique. They are capable of turning the helm for worse by their selfishness, or for good by their renewed insight. Our willingness to suffer at the hands of those responsible persons is a testimony of respect for them. Sometimes such suffering is the only way we can communicate to the key decision-makers an awareness of their responsibility for what they are letting be done to those whom they oppress. It may also be the only way to show them what they do to themselves by being oppressors.

The Underlying Axiom

It is axiomatic for the personalist that the problems of historical structures cannot be solved on the level of historical structures. This is not where the evil lies. We therefore accept (as everyone else must do in their own framework as well) that it is not possible to solve all problems. Redemptive personalism will not agree that its rightness or wrongness is to be measured by whether it can solve them all. No other position can do that either. All problems could be solved, however, if people would let their hearts be touched. Reaching those hearts is therefore the most significant task, even if there will be many cases where it cannot be done.

Shortcomings

This position has serious shortcomings as a social strategy. Its willingness to accept working only from below is at best slow and sometimes defeatist. The trust which it places in the possibility of winning persons is easily mistaken for an ungrounded trust in the inherent redeemability of human nature. If this trust be thought to be rooted in fact, the position will be undermined at the first experiences of radical evil. The position therefore can be held only by those for whom it is deeply rooted in some ground of faith beyond experience.

This position is in danger of being philosophically subservient to a particular view of human personality. It may give up too easily on the structures of society, or it may hope too easily in the possibility of their being completely turned around by the conversion of the person bearing responsibility at the top.

Nevertheless

Nevertheless, there is no alternative to personalism. What cannot be done by persons will not be done. Overarching structures and institutions may amplify or dampen, twist or straighten what people do, but still people will do it. This position is both more realistic and more promising than one which assumes that persons are of no significance, and that the movement of history is a machine in which institutional forces impersonally push one another around. The word for that assumption is *despair,* even if it calls itself realism.

The humanization of personal experience demands that we run the risk of trusting personality even where this risk is objectively not justified. The only alternative is to run our society even farther into the ground by gambling on the assumption that impersonal forces are the most valid and the most powerful.

After All

Although recourse to war is often justified by appeal to nonpersonalistic categories, especially to nonpersonal ways of conceiving of the enemy, yet in the *waging* of war there is a great element of personalism. Often a personality cult is reflected in the larger-than-life stature given to key military personages by journalism and then by memoirs. Historians of war and diplomacy are fond of digging out the moment when the outcome of a particular battle, or even the whole course of a war, was settled by one man's momentary emotional state.[4] There is in the military enterprise also a strong personalistic concern to "win the hearts of the people." Sometimes officers call for firmness and sometimes for benevolence in the "pacification" process to win the respect and the trust of an occupied population.

13

The Pacifism of Cultic Law

The Noncombatants. While recognizing that warfare is unavoidable in maintaining civil government in a world of sin, noncombatants conscientiously object to taking human life. They do not, however, condemn those who take part in war. On the other hand, noncombatants are willing to aid their government in every consistent way in time of warfare, except by taking human life.
—"Seventh-Day Adventists and Civil Government," in
Instruction and Information Manual

According to one stream of current usage, the term *cultic* refers to a position taken on grounds that seek no reasonable explanation, where neither results nor causes, general principles nor motivations are calculated. A "cultic" position is taken simply on the grounds that it must be taken, that the demand for it has been revealed as such, without linking the judgment into a larger system of meanings and values.

This kind of pacifism may, for instance, seek to be totally obedient to the biblical prohibition of the shedding of blood, whether this be thought of as specifically stated in the sixth commandment or otherwise. The obligation is absolute, but it is also arbitrary. One can, like the Seventh-Day Adventists,[1] refuse to kill with one's own hands and yet be willing to participate in the military enterprise, since it is only the act of oneself doing the killing which is forbidden.

The Axiom

Underlying this position is the belief that if we properly interpret revelation as the basis of obedience, there is no room for calculating or interpreting. There is not even any reason to try to discern underlying principles (as in chapter 3, above) and to obey them consistently. Ours is only the task of keeping the rules clearly. For those matters to which the revelation has not spoken, we do no necessary service to God by trying to extend the principles we have been given or to make deductions from them.

Shortcomings

There are serious disadvantages to the position, which come to the surface even more clearly than in the somewhat similar case of "revealed principles." The process of internal testing enables one genuinely to appropriate an ethical position, making it one's own so that one can confidently live within it. But this is undermined if we are to ask for no explanations and applications, if ethical obligation is arbitrary. Nor is it clear what kind of message one has to the outside world of those who have not chosen to listen to our peculiar source of specific instructions.

Nevertheless

Like the positions of absolute principle and absolute conscience, this immature vision of the nature of ethical obligation may constitute a valid shortcut on the path from the general to the particular. Some communities and persons do not have or take the luxury and leisure of working through all the intellectual dimensions of a decision. If moral guides are to be accepted in implicit faith, then let us rejoice if they are rules which foster reverence for life.

After All

The only alternative to a cultic moralism which reverences life seems to be the equally cultic, arbitrary, unaccountable, and ungeneralizable obligations of patriotism. That is probably the only alternative for persons who make decisions on a cultic level. Note how the guerrilla efforts of Che Guevara in Bolivia or of "freedom fighters" in many situations of turmoil are evaluated morally by their supporters. This often has about it this same kind of unconcern for efficacy, accountability, morality.

The imperative of the battle is self-sustaining. Its transcendental rootage is subject to no critique. If the cultic rule which I impose upon myself is an abstention from killing, it at least does not actively and institutionally go about sacrificing others to my irrational commitment, as does most warfare.

14

The Pacifism of Cultural Isolation

Our family has always been Mennonite. We have never taken part in war. That is because we have nothing to do with the world and its ways. It has nothing to do with us what the world does. It would go contrary to our forefathers to go to war.
—Old Colony Mennonite

Where did we ever get the idea that the powers that be (Rom. 13:1-4) are directed by kingdom rules? . . . Let's not criticize our Maker for having one set of rules for the people of his kingdom and another set of rules for the powers that be.
—Menno D. Sell, letter to *Gospel Herald*[1]

It is quite possible for a segregated social group to feel so much at home in its own subcivilization and so alienated from the larger society that the concerns and values of the larger society have no attraction or obligation. There is thus no self-evident duty to defend what the larger society is defending, to be in favor of its political order, or to be willing to fight for its freedom.

Every ethnic group has its own particular language and

cooking and style of life. It just happens to be the cultural peculiarity of some Mennonites,[2] who have in many different times and places avoided military service. Toward this end they emigrated from countries which introduced universal military training—from Prussian lands in the 1780s, from Russia and from Alsace in the 1870s. Like the plain coat, the buggy, or their Germanic dialects, the practice of refusing military service has come to be sacred through the many generations of its association with the Mennonite culture.

Yet it is not usually held by such minorities that theirs is the only possible position for Christians to take. A member of the in-group would hesitate to expect Mennonite behavior of anyone not part of the ethnic group. One would in many cases not want to suggest that a non-Mennonite who does not share the nonresistant position is any less Christian. From within this view, it would seem incongruous if any significant numbers of persons without Mennonite upbringing were to find the Mennonite ethos convincing.

The Axiom

Underlying this position is the belief that one accepts one's own distinctive identity, family, and culture as a divine gift. To be a person is to be local, parochial, and provincial.[3] This local identity is to be received with thanks as a gift from God, to be cherished, not despite the fact that it is strange, but precisely because it is a rare and curious heritage.

Shortcomings

This position, however, recognizes no missionary responsibility to the world around. It gives up on any possible wider acceptance of its own position. The same reasons which keep its own members faithful within the separate culture will normally be expected to operate in keeping those outside just as faithful within their nationalistic, militaristic frame of life.

A further practical weakness of this position is the crumbling of the cultural barriers of the isolated community in the face of population growth and urbanization. The subgroup finds it increasingly difficult to maintain enough contact with the developed world to market agricultural goods and buy a necessary minimum of manufactured goods, without becoming open to cultural accommodation as well.

Nevertheless

Yet everyone to be human must to some degree accept one's born particularity and limitations. Any wider world to which one might prefer to escape is equally particular and provincial, just on a larger scale. There is no Christian community, and there is no wider humanity, which is not thus provincial. The Amish and Hutterian subcultures just might be the most viable self-sufficient communities left in the West, outside the mainstream melting pot, able to survive when the fossil fuel will have run out.

After All

Such a provincialism eschews violence and renounces any imposition of its own standards on others—even of its Christian standards on other Christians. It is to be preferred to the violent provincialism of warriors, ready to destroy others to defend their own apartness. None have more irrevocably given up on the world outside their ingroup than those who are willing to destroy a portion of that wider world.

15

The Pacifism of Consistent Nonconformity

"Because not for us is the wrestling against blood and flesh." Nothing could be plainer than that it is a general principle for life that earthly combat and struggle is never the portion of the Christian disciple. One could as well argue that the command for the children to obey their parents only applies on Sunday, as to claim that spiritual warfare applies only to spiritual activities.
—James R. Graham, *Strangers and Pilgrims*

The socially dualist Mennonites and the Hutterian Brethren are not merely isolated (chapter 14). Their apartness may also be taken as the most appropriate Protestant example of a rejection of military force, derived from a still more sweeping and still more basic rejection of the world in all its forms. The military is not simply an instrument for killing if necessary. It is also the quintessence of most other sins: theft, deceit, adultery, pride, pomp, and power hunger.[1]

The demand for military service is the point at which the surrounding world most pressingly reaches into the life of the separate community. The world systematically and vigorously seeks to change the character and lifestyle of that group. At this point it is self-evident that the person committed to a life of nonconformity to the world must see the demand for separation focused in its starkest form.

The Old Order Amish Mennonite or the Hutterite rejection of participation in the military is rooted within a deeper sweeping nonconformity. This rootage completely liberates them from any obligation to explain how they would run the world without force, how they would solve the problems which violence does not solve, defend their families, etc. They have chosen the better part. It is not for them to dictate or even to suggest how those whose spiritual loyalty is to the values of this world could achieve their own ends without using their own violent means.

They may follow the logic of their social dualism so far as to say that what is "wrong" for them might be "right" for others.[2] Or they may simply suspend judgment. In either case, the worldings' problems and needs, the distress and the defense of the larger society—these are none of their concern.

The Axiom

Underlying this position is the stance that to begin with, we must reckon with the reality of the "world," in the radically rebellious sense of that term which is characteristic of the usage of the New Testament's general epistles and John's Gospel. This world is not simply a state of mind but an empirical network of institutions and ways of behaving. It has as its definition its rebellion against the will of God and its self-glorification. Being an empirical, evil reality, it can be seen and must be shunned. Any witness to it, any missionary presence in its midst, must be secondary to the duty first of all for the consistent nonconformist to identify it and take a stance over against it.

Shortcomings

This is a position with some evident ethical disadvantages. It is, however, not proper to condemn it as hastily as many do. It is not expressive of a consistent rejection of the world or opposition between *Christ and Culture.*[3] This is the most illogical misinterpretation.

Consistent nonconformity discerns worldliness as a cultural reality and identifies those worldly cultural practices which are to be avoided. Precisely because of this, it is more committed than any other stance to creating a Christian cultural alternative to the world. This is immediately evident in any survey of the ways in which, ever since the sixteenth century, Hutterian and Amish separate communities have been culturally creative.

These communities have succeeded beyond any other comparable populations in creating and maintaining a nearly self-sufficient civilization. They have their own mores, characterized by love for the land and efficient use of it, craftsmanship, strongly supportive social relations, nonviolent sanctions for deviants, and their own solutions to the problems of survival and identity.

Over against the depersonalizing effects of mass education, they have created not a culture vacuum but an alternative pattern of transmission and value definition. In case of disaster, this just might be the only subculture capable of surviving in North America outside the mainstream or without the mainstream. Whatever is wrong with the Amish and Hutterian patterns, it is not that they are against culture.

The real disadvantage is rather a fruit of their cultural strength. This community recreates itself in its progeny. As a result, within a few generations numerous members in the church are committed only superficially or grudgingly to its values. There thus comes to be "world" inside the church. With growing awareness of other Christian groups, one cannot avoid recognizing as well that there is also "church" outside in the world. But such a recognition must seriously undermine the group's confidence in its own mission.

Yet the deeper flaw is the way in which such a systematic rejection of the wider world becomes a hidden dependence upon it. Whatever the outside society does, one must do otherwise. Thereby the church is dependent upon the world which it rejects, in that the world is permitted to dictate the patterns of its rejection.

Nevertheless

Yet it is the case that war is eminently representative of the structured insurrection of humankind against the loving will of God. There is such a thing as a fallen cosmos which the Christian should not love (1 John 2:15), and the sword is characteristic of it. Fratricide is the first sin in Genesis 4 and the primary example of sin in 1 John 3. Jesus was tempted more by violence than he was by sloth, gluttony, lust, and other standard sins. War is the only sin in which the result is so irrevocable; other sins may destroy the one sinned against, while killing always does.

After All

The same type of monolithic thinking about the world tends to prevail on the conformist side as well. Some Christians accept war in principle because of a decision of principle to "accept the world" and because acceptance of the world on its own terms is in all circumstances the best thing to do. These are the so-called "hard Niebuhrians."[4] They tend to be the least capable of discriminating moral judgment within that involvement. There is then a categorical decision to accept the wrong in the world on its own terms.

If we take war as the eminent example of this acceptance of the world, such persons are even less morally free, and even less realistic about the power of sin, than are systematic nonconformists.

16

The Nonpacifist Nonresistance of the Mennonite "Second Wind"

The term nonresistance *as commonly used today describes the faith and life of those who accept the Scriptures as the revealed will of God, and who cannot have any part in warfare because they believe the Bible forbids it, and who renounce all coercion, even nonviolent coercion. Pacifism, on the other hand, is a term which covers many types of opposition to war. Some modern pacifists are opposed to all wars, and some are not. Some who oppose all wars find their authority in the will of God, while others find it largely in human reason.*
—Guy F. Hershberger, *War, Peace, and Nonresistance*

Thus far in this survey of the logically possible options, I have not generally sought to be representative of denominational experience. I have not labeled some positions as Catholic and some as Quaker, though in some cases I could have. Seldom is a particular denomination, at least for long, representative of only one line of interpretation.

There is, however, one contemporary exception to this generalization. One particular movement in recent North American Mennonite experience has developed a specific new understanding in response to its leaders' encounter with other currents of thought. The problem which surfaces here is worthy of observation beyond the limits of the denomination. The reason for commenting on this type of pacifism is not that I assume the reading audience to be Mennonite. Nor is it an attempt on my part to speak for or against a part of my own tradition. Instead, in keeping with the purpose of the book as a whole, I include this position because it has come to be known and used as an ideal type far beyond the bounds of its own confession.

Already on the surface of language usage the problem is visible: the word pacifism itself became a subject of controversy among denominational leaders during World War II. This can be illustrated simply by comparing the texts written by leading denominational thinkers in the past generation.

John R. Mumaw, then a Bible teacher and later president at Eastern Mennonite College, wrote in the midst of World War II a pamphlet, *Nonresistance and Pacifism,*[1] in which he strongly presented the argument that the position taken by Mennonites with regard to war, traditionally labeled as nonresistance, has little in common with the modern Protestant phenomenon known as pacifism, especially in the World Wars.

Beside it we may place the article, "The Pacifism of the Sixteenth-Century Anabaptists," read to the American Society of Church History in December 1954 by the denomination's then most prominent historian, Harold S. Bender.[2]

These two qualified denominational teachers were describing what they would both have testified was basically the same position. One of them accepted as an identification of this position the label "pacifism," to which he then gave specific content out of Mennonite history. The other began by assuming that the same word, in the usage of others, already had a contemporary meaning, designating a position he rejected. Instead of trying to redeem the word by giving it his own proper meaning, he preferred to reject it.

Probably due to the cultural image of Mennonitism in the public mind, the usage favored by Professor Mumaw was most widely perceived beyond the denomination. John C. Bennett considered Mennonitism as paradigmatic for what he called a "strategy of withdrawal."[3] Thomas Sanders took the same line with the characterization "apolitical."[4] Mennonites are a pure type and represent one possible position with great integrity.

Something similar happened, for other reasons, within the denomination as well. This matter of vocabulary brought to the surface a long-simmering problem of cultural and theological identity. American Mennonites first began to seek to communicate to the English-speaking world around them, just before, during, and after World War I. As they did so, the temptation was natural to identify naively with any kind of available peace position over against all kinds of militarism and nationalism. In this connection they had a certain sympathy for the antiwar movements of the period between the first two World Wars. To this experience we owe the acceptance of the phrases "historic peace churches" and "peace witness."

But then there came a serious second look. Most Mennonites were powerfully impressed by the differences which separated them from the pacifisms of the Peace Pledge Union and the Fellowship of Reconciliation. Some of the positions taken by those pacifists were not specifically Christian in their orientation. Some of them placed so much trust in the goodness of human nature that they had not faced the deep need for suffering in the cause of divine love. Some were not ready to pay the price for full consistency in the rejection of all war. Some were unjustifiably optimistic about the capacity of an unregenerate society to solve its problems without breakage.

They seemed to promise a changed motivation, suggesting that war could be abolished by fiat. They failed to recognize the moral compromise in their own willingness to resort to nonviolent types of coercion, or to make exceptions for an international "peace-keeping" army. In their optimism about doing away with violence within a society, they failed to observe that the threat of force is part of what keeps the peace.

In the rebound from this discovery of clear differences, some Mennonites then reversed their orientation. They came to conclude that except within a nonresistant separated church, there is no foundation at all for nonresistance. Hence, in some sense at least, war is "right for the government although it is wrong for us."[5]

This kind of thinking was favored by the desire to be somehow intellectually acceptable. It was suggested by thinkers like Reinhold Niebuhr, who were willing to recognize Mennonites as being right in their place, as having understood Jesus well. In return, such thinkers wanted Mennonites to grant that war is somehow right for governments. Or in other cases, the mainstream position to which one conformed was that of a more traditional Protestant orthodoxy. That taught a separately revealed set of moral obligations for government, different from those binding upon the individual Christian.

This temptation to ethical dualism was favored in addition by the cultural accommodation through which American Mennonites had gone in the last few generations. If one limits nonresistance to oneself, one can then be nonresistant and still patriotic and anticommunist. One can be accepted within denominational pluralism and within patriotic small-town society without representing much challenge to the beliefs of others. One can live up to one's own rules, respect the dictates of one's own conscience for oneself, and also accept that others must live by other rules. This is an especially attractive temptation for those who had already partly slipped into the understandings of the meaning of their stance which we have described above as "cultic" or "cultural" or separated (see above, chapters 13–15).

Another thrust in the same direction was Mennonite involvement in the fundamentalist controversies of this same epoch. Critical modern theologies could write off the holy wars of the Old Testament as due to the primitive culture of the time and therefore not relevant today. Mennonites could not so easily forget Joshua and Deborah and David. It was simpler to set the Old Testament–New Testament tension parallel to the world-church tension. Capital punishment and war are proper for the Israelites, and for the world, but not for New Testament Christians.[6]

There thus arose a newly respectable systematic ethical dualism. Many Mennonites preferred to call their position "nonresistance" (following Matthew 5:39, "Do not resist").[7] They were concerned carefully to distinguish it from pacifism in general and from nonviolent activism in particular. Some Mennonites since 1940 have thus invested as much concern in keeping their distance from pacifism as they have in denouncing militarism. In fact, in this view, the military have their place in the non-Christian world, and some Mennonites commend the violence of the state, as long as they need not be a part of it.

The Unspoken Axiom

The thought underlying this position would seem to be double. Socially, it assumes that if you are complimented on your integrity, you should accept the compliment. The Niebuhrian analysis, while rejecting the sectarian position as proud and irresponsible, concedes to it both that it is consistent and that it understands Jesus aright. Rather than looking twice to test the sincerity or the hidden assumptions of such a backhanded compliment, dualistic Mennonites, gratified for a place in the sun even if it be under a shadow, accepted the challenge and set out trying to be consistently apolitical.[8]

Intellectually, this view assumes that a clear division of labor between two realms or worlds or levels is a step forward in understanding. Once this is done, you need only ask of each moral issue in which area it lies, and the problem is solved.

Shortcomings

There are several kinds of deficiencies in this position. One type arises from the fact of its recent origins in efforts to fasten upon Mennonitism a structure of interpretation borrowed from its critics, rather than one growing out of its own experience. The analysis does not fit. It hides from Mennonites the broad (conservative) political meaning of their participation in the national economy, in educational and professional life.

This view also overlooks the (critical) political impact of Mennonites' freedom to emigrate, their conscientious objection, their service agencies, their church schools, their alternative community. It leads them to deny their real sympathies for specific political options and for outspokenly religious statesmen. They cannot feel comfortable in applying to active churchmen in high places (John Foster Dulles, Mark Hatfield, George McGovern) an analysis whose original axiom was that the state is pagan.

But the weakness of this view is not only that it does not fit the life of the group it seeks to represent. It is equally questionable on other grounds as well. It implicitly denies both missionary and ecumenical concern, since in effect "Christ is Lord for us but not for them." It accepts as if it were a compliment the judgment of political irrelevance pronounced by establishment theologians not only on "sectarians" but also thereby on Jesus. It makes of Jesus neither a good man nor a prophet but a cardboard figure outside the real world. It concedes to government—though somehow seldom to other governments than our own—a mandate to wage war which goes far beyond the substance of the New Testament view of the state.[9]

Often this position mixes in the theocratic imagery of the Old Testament holy wars, as if every modern government were somehow an equivalent of ancient Israel. It hastily denies inherent close relations Mennonites could well have to other peace movements, on grounds of criticisms (humanistic optimism, irrealism about sin and power) which would apply even more to military alternatives.

This view also fails to recognize that any known militarism in the real world shares all the vices of non-Christian pacifism. Militarism as well as pacifism is humanistic and utopian. It places enormous trust in the wisdom of administrative bureaucracy, in the moral insight of persons who have been hardened to think of other men as worthy of extermination. Shall we entrust peace and freedom to the military establishment? Shall we trust a person with powerful weapons to be morally self-critical? That places greater and more unjustified confidence in human character than does any kind of pacifism. Every kind of trust in weapons is just as non-Christian in its moral assumptions and certainly more unchristian in its activities than the comparable types of humanistically overconfident pacifism.

Nevertheless

This view may well claim the pastoral and pedagogical merits of the cultic and isolation views (chapters 13-15, above) whose weaknesses it shares as well. Its radical simplification makes it possible for a religious community to survive and to understand itself in lay language.

Suppose it really is (or when and where it concretely should be) the case that immediate political relevance is accessible only at the cost of abandoning faithfulness to Jesus' word and example. Then the disciple of Jesus will certainly choose faithfulness even at the cost of withdrawal. Such a placement of the alternatives, however, is itself not according to the gospel, nor is the assumed definition of "relevance" underlying it. This is where the "apolitical" Mennonite has been misled. But once the question is thus posed (by the ecumenical interlocutor), the sectarian answer is the better one of the two options the Mennonite has been given.

After All

Every possible way of justifying war also introduces a similar radical dualism. According to that, what is wrong elsewhere is right in war. The theological mainstream agrees that one cannot face the politician's problems and follow Jesus, in the way he said he wanted to be followed, according to the Gospels. As naive, unmissionary, and potentially self-righteous as this neo-Mennonite ethical dualism is, it is still less so than the alternative it rejects.

17

And On and On . . .

The list above may seem long enough, and perhaps it is, if our goal was merely to dramatize the multiplicity of logics that may move people to renounce war. Yet let us not think that the list is complete. There are noteworthy persons, traditions, and movements which would not yet find themselves fairly represented by any one or any combination of the above statements. Without providing for each an analysis as long as those proffered above, we may still recognize the presence of remaining gaps by adding a few briefer characterizations.

A. The Pacifism of the Eschatological Parenthesis

This position is represented today by Jehovah's Witnesses and by some dispensationalist Protestants. In the sixteenth century Melchior Hofmann and perhaps Hans Hut thought this way. It has some basis in the apocalyptic literature of the biblical age.

There is a change coming soon in world history, it affirms, which will divide that history into two portions. The present "dispensation" or period in history is a parenthetical one in which the will of God for his people is "faithfulness" in suffering. But after the imminent inbreak of the new regime, the rules will change. God will destroy his enemies. And God may well make use of his faithful people in that judgment.

The rejection of warfare in the present is then not the application of a generally nonviolent set of always applicable ethical principles. To be guided by such principles without regard to time would be to deny God's governing freedom. God prescribes for each age a pattern of faithfulness which is not calculating but simply obedient. It is not ours to reason why, but it is ours in this age to be ready to die. No kind of calculation or justification of behavior in terms of motive or effectiveness is relevant. God has prescribed the where and the when of our suffering now and of our triumph soon. Those who share now in his long-suffering with rebellious humanity will one day share in the triumph of Armageddon.

Incidentally, it is possible for this parenthetical logic to work the other way around just as well. Logically, this should not surprise us, since the shifting of regimes from one age to the next is not according to human reason, but dictated by divine sovereignty. The *Scofield Reference Bible*, probably the most widely read current medium for this view, reserves the ethic of the Sermon on the Mount, with the command to love our enemies, to a future "Kingdom age."[1] The Sermon is not binding for the present age because "the Jews" of the first century did not accept Jesus as King.

B. Anarchic Pacifism[2]

A kind of pacifism, generally referred to as anarchic, is represented in the 1960s by youth within movements like Students for a Democratic Society.[3] Their sense of the meaning of social movement is such that the most needed social contribution is to obstruct the functioning of the existing evil establishment. Protesters do not feel it is their responsibility to assure the availability of a better alternative structure or solution, or even to guarantee that their own interference will be productive. The only criterion is radical disavowal of the present.

Such anarchists assume that if the present system is forced to grind to a halt, then anything else that can come next would certainly be better. The rhetoric may speak of taking responsibility, but this does not involve projecting and then implementing a clear alternative strategy, available and waiting to be put into effect after the seizure of power. To offer that kind of cure would be a contradiction in terms. This position is a pacifism in that the military establishment is near the center of what it disavows. It is, however, not a complete alternative social program, but rather an unstable or impermanent mixture of utopianism (chapter 8, above), nonviolent direct action (5), and just war (2).

C. The Pacifism of Consistent Self-Negation

There may be such a thing as a consistent Asian pacifism of self-negation. If all outward human history is either illusion or inexorable impersonal necessity, if my own individual living is no grounds for hope, if my goal is blessed release from the treadmill of life and from desire, if the acceptance of suffering for its own sake or as a spiritual discipline is one of the highest goals, if contradiction can never be disentangled into clean yes-or-no options—then what is worth fighting for?

The ends which are called on to justify war fade away in the concrete social and political despair in which Asian humanity lives. Or such goals evaporate in the misty light of the religions whose call to people is that by accepting hopelessness they can find release from deceptive desire. There is a clear element of caricature in this description. It is a capsule statement of how the East is sometimes perceived by an uncomprehending West. Nonetheless, even in caricatured form this perspective remains significant. It may stand as a critique of the compulsiveness with which Westerners are convinced they must bring about righteous ends, soon, by their own power.

D. The Pacifism of the Very Long View

Others arrive at a pacifism by taking a very long view of human affairs. All of the discussions about what must be averted by war point to an evil which is likely to take place in the near future. Yet we should have learned by now that short-range appearances often deceive. The long-range movement of history is regularly determined by factors quite different from those which dominate the consciousness of those who think they are making crucial decisions.

All political reality is morally ambiguous. However sure we are about the relatively greater justice of a given cause, the difference cannot be so much as to justify the absolute recourse which war represents. We know so little about how things will turn out. Any impatient preoccupation with insuring the right short-range results may be condemned, not because it breaks some moral law, but because it is shortsighted and impatient.

There is a form of pacifist argument which says that the aggressor and the defender are morally not very different because both are using violence. Reinhold Niebuhr answered this long ago: "There is a perspective from which there is not much difference between my egotism and that of a gangster. But from another perspective there is an important difference."[4] The fact that both are selfish does not make them morally equivalent. The "selfishness" which defends the innocent is better than the selfishness of the aggressor.

Of course! But in the "sober long view" described here, the difference that matters (if we speak of war) is not between the gangster and myself, or between policeman and criminal, but between two policemen or between two gangsters. This brings us to the special danger—to which Reinhold Niebuhr elsewhere pointed with clarity—that in pride and insensitivity to criticism, a self-righteous policeman may well be worse than a gangster.

The loss of sovereignty might just be the way to survive. Ponder the experience of the Czechs in 1968, the Danes in 1940, the inhabitants of the Gaza Strip in 1968, or the Dominican Republic under the American invasion of 1966, the Poles in 1980. None of these subject peoples could choose the option of heroic resistance, in any form other than that of surrender. In these cases the loss of national sovereignty may actually be the occasion for a renewal and revitalization of national identity, which often thrives under foreign occupation.[5] Even more is it possible that the suffering or subjection of a people, in a setting where there could be no thought of some heroic uprising, may be an occasion for growth and renewal in the Christian church.

A close relative of this long-view pacifism is the modesty concern. Power is arrogant and corrupts its bearer. The claim to set the world right undercuts itself. This can be said theologically in terms of idolatry, or in sober political science in terms of arrogance. It is not a mere spiritual pastoral counsel: "Too much power goes to your head." It is rather a political mechanism. Whoever claims to impose righteous order on the rest of the world is actually a tyrant.

E. The Pacifism of Redemptive Suffering

There may be a distinct and coherent pacifism of redemptive suffering. The willing acceptance of suffering is a part of the Gandhian method[6] and of the Anabaptist[7] and Mennonite nonresistant traditions. For the Gandhian, the suffering is conceived as instrumental. It contributes to an effect upon the powerful. It is the price of nonviolent resistance, or it is a way to touch the heart. For others, the suffering itself may be seen as bringing about a healing or purgative effect in society, or expiation in the mystical order of things.

At least about the distant past, we are often able to say

that tragedy had its fruitfulness. This is a possible generalization about suffering in history. It is a necessary Christian affirmation about certain kinds of suffering.

F. The Imitation of Jesus

Some have held to the ancient ethical tradition of the imitation of Jesus. It makes the same moral claims as the pacifism of moral law (type 3, above), yet its content is not abstract commands but rather the life and word of Jesus. His command and example are to be followed without calculation of social possibilities. Its major spokespersons have been Peter Waldo, Petr Chelčický,[8] and Leo Tolstoy. It does not expect widespread acceptance, but neither does it acquiesce in the world's noncompliance with Jesus' norm, as do the other minority approaches (types 9 and 12-15, above).

G. The Pacifism of Self-Discipline

In this pacifism, the center of moral obligation may be located in my responsibility to discipline myself. I may forbid myself to kill, or I may refuse to participate in the military machine. Not because I cannot bring myself to hate and to kill, but because I can bring myself to do it too easily. My propensity to hatred and to violence makes me aware that, if I am to be human, I need at this point to govern and tame the very forces which the military life unleashes and glorifies.

In this connection, then, the logic does not center upon the action itself but upon my responsibility for the kind of person I make myself by what I do. This differs from the virtuous minority approach (type 9) by its individualism, from the utopian (8) by its concrete self-discipline, from the personalist (12) by its being more concerned for the evil in one's self than for the adversary. It is compatible with the moral absolute (3) and absolute conscience (11) approaches, but more flexible in its psychological awareness.

H. Situational Pacifism

Two or three fads ago, Americans were reading paperbacks on ethics by Joseph Fletcher, James Pike, and others, advocating what they (incorrectly) called "a new morality." They argued the need for moral decision to take into account the specific situation. Then they exemplified the decision process with abundant anecdotal illustrations of times when it seemed that one would simply have to do something that was against the rules. They argued that the decision-in-the-situation is a distinct, and a correct, mode of ethical reasoning.

As ethical approaches go, this one turned out to be most unhelpful. Every case of "simply have to" turns out on logical analysis to be just another rule, albeit an unavowed one. To explain why one must do what seemed to be forbidden by one rule, there is no argument that does not point to another ethical generalization about values which, one claims, is (not always, but in this situation) of greater weight.

Nonetheless, the currency of this contextualist rhetoric does loosen up ethical discourse. As a result, some who reject firm moral generalizations are willing to take positions against war on visceral or intuitional grounds, or on unconscious casuistic grounds (like type 2, above). They are unable to explain or feel no need to articulate these positions responsibly. They may even think it would be wrong to generalize from particular cases. Thus they may reject a given war, at a given time, for themselves, without sensing any duty to test the validity of their arguments by measuring other wars or challenging the decisions of other people.

18

And Then On and On Some More . . .

I have come back to this conversation after two decades, asked by readers and editors to update my outline in the light of how the world has been changing. Now I have had to ask whether there are any things which I have learned which do not fit simply into the chinks of the text as I wrote it in 1970. To be fair to the material, I should add a few more compartments. I add them here, after the first stocktaking of chapter 17, and before my own conclusions (now renumbered as chapters 19 and 20). Thus the reader can most easily see what they add to the picture.

A. The Pacifism of Rabbinic Monotheism

Not until I had been studying for decades in the field of *Christian* pacifism did I discover to what extent Christian pacifist convictions had been foreshadowed in the Jewish experience of Jews since Jeremiah. This is one of the gaps in my own education for which I least easily can forgive my teachers. The anti-Jewish tilt in most Christian self-definition had made it seem that, for the pacifism of Jesus to be coherent, he must have defined it over against a non-pacifist background. It also seemed that for the Christians of the second century to be nonviolent, the Jews of that same time must have been violent. This way of taking the story is radically wrong.

I renounce the effort to spread the story of Jewish pacifism across the grid of my 1970 outline; it is too complex and would not fit well into the same dialectical format. I must limit myself to a simpler outline format.[1] Here are some of the basic *underlying axioms:*

1. Radical Monotheism. There is one God, all-wise, all-good, and all-powerful. We are not in charge of the world and should not seek to be, since God is. God can protect whom he will; if we seek to defend ourselves, we lack trust in his care. Good will triumph in God's own time and by his doing. If we suffer, God may be using us to "sanctify his name" (as martyrs), or he may be chastising us for our sin. In all of these ways, letting God be God undercuts the case for our trying to take charge of the course of history by means of righteous violence.

2. Disillusionment with Royalty. From Saul to Josiah, Israel gave kingship after the model of their neighbors a good test, an experiment, and God let them try it. Then God moved, most clearly in the message of Jeremiah, to an alternative vision of the calling of his people to a mission among the nations. Thrice[2] violent efforts to restore royalty failed, indicating that that was not God's way. Since Jeremiah on a world scale and since Bar Kochba even in the former land of Israel, nonviolence is the normative Jewish moral vision.[3] We have been misled by Christian antisemitism (and recently by Zionism) into missing that fact.

3. Minority Survival. Gentile oppressors are here to stay, but with political realism it is possible to survive among them, even to prosper. Joseph, Esther, and Daniel are the prototypes of faithful Jews who, by being faithful under duress, honored God and were protected. The relative "peace" of such a minority existence is preferable to any recourse to violence.

4. Avoiding Idolatry. God is "jealous": the worship of any other "gods" is intolerable. Yet every Gentile nation and every Gentile army is held together by idolatry. Military service was inseparable from worship.

5. God's Covenant Law. God as moral legislator abhors bloodshed. The first social sin in Genesis (chap. 4) was fratricide; God condemned the sin but saved the killer's life. The only social demand of the covenant with Noah (chap. 9) was to abstain from bloodshed.

6. One God Reigns. Since there is only one God ruling the whole universe, other peoples and even their governments have a place in God's plan.

All of the above characteristics of Judaism were present in the first century of our era and were taken over unquestioningly by the first Christians. None of them, however, is specific to Christian faith; all of them continued to characterize nonmessianic Jewish thought as well.[4] The rabbis over the centuries reinforced all of them, but especially strands 1, 2, and 5.

A Shortcoming

The Jewish heritage, in the eyes of many Jews in our time, too easily made its peace with subjugation and second-class status. Although in times of relative prosperity Jews could expertly negotiate their way around rulers and other social groups, they were unable to fight back and sometimes even unable to escape when the pogroms came. When measured by the modern Western visions of national dignity, this appears to be an unworthy fate for God's people.

Nevertheless

Yet the faith community which can survive in dispersion is a stronger social phenomenon than the empire which depends on a central dictatorship. First in the Middle East and then in Europe, the Jews have outlived dozens of "eternal" empires and dynasties "by divine right." A faith community gathered around a book and a prophetic proclamation, needing no temple or priesthood, is more resilient and more able to sustain its character than are the Gentile alternatives. For two and a half millennia, from Josiah to Ben Gurion, Jewry represents the longest and strongest experience of religious-cultural-moral continuity in known history, defended without the sword.

B. The Pacifism of the Coherent Cosmos: Making Means Fit Ends

The most powerful and perhaps the simplest argument in the field, in our century, was the response of Gandhi to the question whether a good objective does not justify even an evil deed. "Why should we not obtain our goal, which is good, by any means whatever, even by using violence?"[5] His answer was that means and ends cannot thus be separated: "Your belief that there is no connection between the means and the end is a great mistake. . . . The means may be likened to a seed, the end to a tree; and there is just the same inviolable connection between the means and the end as there is between the seed and the tree."

Gandhi goes on to argue by means of hypothetical scenarios, but it is clear that his case is not based upon them. His case is based upon a conviction regarding the organic unity of the cosmos, whereby evil seed can never yield good fruit. His synthesis of the Christian and Hindu moral visions could draw this conviction from both sides.

Martin Luther King, Jr., made the same point in a quite different way. Called often to respond to the objection that nonviolent action was not sure to succeed, he fell back on old and new formulations of the Christian hope. The old ones were the African-American Baptist version of the New Testament promise of a coming kingdom. The New England counterpart was the poem by James Russell Lowell which he quoted from the platform as often as any:

> Though the cause of evil prosper,
> Yet 'tis Truth alone is strong. . . .
> Truth forever on the scaffold,
> Wrong forever on the throne—
> Yet that scaffold sways the future,
> And, behind the dim unknown,
> Standeth God within the shadow,
> Keeping watch above his own.[6]

The Underlying Axiom

Thus in ways that are quite different in wording and imagery but parallel in impact, both Gandhi and King rejected the pragmatic justification of means by ends. They chose a worldview according to which, in the long run, because the cosmos is in the hand of God (despite the presence of sin), we reap what we sow.

Gandhi, King, and their associates made pragmatic calculations of timing, of how symbolic actions communicate, of how the adversary can be given room to move without being permitted to move in the wrong direction. These strategies comprised a large part of their special skill.

Yet pragmatic considerations *alone* were never permitted to justify concessions on the use of violence itself.[7] The ultimate reason they gave for that was not a rigid conception of moral obligation, but the worldview according to which violence is self-defeating. The renunciation of violence, including the acceptance of innocent suffering, is redemptive.[8] We do not renounce the effectiveness which violence offers because it is forbidden, in some religious or philosophical lawbook. We renounce it because in deep reality, in the long run, and on the average, it is not effective but self-defeating.

A Shortcoming

It is a weakness of this position that it is derived from a worldview which people do not have to hold. That innocent suffering is powerful is not easy to believe. Specifically, the bearers of power in our societies do not believe in that view, or they would not oppress as they do. "The masses" might more likely be found, in some cultures, to hold some such residual faith in the moral coherence of the cosmos. But most of their children will have been brainwashed otherwise by the common currency of the global village. The overarching systems which used to hold life and the world together in a tradition-rooted culture have by now in most places lost their taken-for-granted power to convince, and soon will have lost it everywhere else.

Nevertheless

Yet that is only a final blow if we ourselves do not believe. The confidence in the coherence of the moral universe is not something these men invented in order to move people to follow them. Instead, it is the presence of that conviction at the root of our religious culture, alive even when under attack by the acids of enlightenment, which swept both Gandhi and King into events larger than they themselves had dreamed.

After All

Any cause for which people in large numbers are willing to kill also claims that there is something about the universe which tends toward justice.[9] They too claim that public moral choice cannot be reduced to pragmatic effectiveness; they too speak of noble sacrifice in the interest of a New World Order.

C. The Pacifist Thrust of Anarchism[10]

We observed above, as a subset of the just-war family, the notion that while war is always wrong, violent defense of the innocent is not. In other words, the several levels of the question which "the state" represents are separated from one another and dealt with differently.

Now we turn to a view which broadens the question instead of narrowing it. What is to be called into question is not the activity of government in war, but all government. In ordinary careful usage, *anarchy* describes a situation in which there is no effective governmental authority. No such situation exists, although there are brief times and places, some brief and some extended, where dominion over a particular society is contested. Anarchism on the other hand is an ism, a vision of how things ought to be.[11] It is a utopian vision; it does not really exist, just as "government of the people, by the people, and for the people" does not really exist.

The Underlying Axiom

For those who project that vision of anarchy,[12] however, it is the best way to make clear their criticism of the illegitimacy of present unjust arrangments. That criticism is little more than carrying to its logical conclusion the critical perspective on the legitimacy of rulers, calling for consent of the governed, going all the way back to the beginnings of democracy. If the way society is administered *really* had my *uncoerced* consent, going beyond being a de facto government to which I had no choice but to yield, then that would not be government (-archy, rule) as we know it. Neither would it be chaos or the war of all against all. Instead, it would be a nondomineering ordering because it is consensual.

An anarchist would not have to be pacifist in the ad hoc grudging adjustment that needs to be made to the present nonideal world. But obviously anarchism *as an ism* must be pacifist, since it offers a utopian vision of how things ought to be. The strongest recent voice in this tone is Vernard Eller's *Christian Anarchy*.[13] A similar argument is just under the surface in Jacques Ellul's *Anarchy and Christianity*.[14]

A Shortcoming

It is hard to converse with this view, since it steps back from the standard criteria for social debate. Feasibility in the present world is not a requirement, since present structures do not meet the requirements of legitimacy.

Persons holding this ideal then have two choices in the real world. They may abstain from formal involvement in "power" of the kind represented by political structures, after the model of the nonparticipation of the early Christians.[15] This would then be like the "neosectarian" dualism described in chapter 16. Or they may develop some notion of compromise, whereby their "involvement" is unavoidable, but never to be justified.[16]

In the former case (abstention) it seems irresponsible, and in the later (compromise) it seems to deny its own prior commitment.

Nevertheless

Yet there is a certain rude consistency in the refusal to make a neat package by arguing a justification for compromise. We cannot deny the rootage in the gospel of the challenge which it addresses to all forms of domination.

After All

The several main streams of people who justify war use arguments in its favor which are just as far from fitting the reality which they in fact support.

D. Being Peaceable: The Pacifism of Virtue

There has been a renewal of attention to the language of *virtue*. This is one of the major changes in the form of the vocation of Christian ethics in the twenty years since this book was first published.[17] Many views seek the crux of morality by centering attention upon the point of decision, where in the face of hard choices, one must choose. Instead, the ethic of virtue asks first who the person is who makes those choices. Often knowing more about that decision-making being can make the choosing less crucial.

As contrasted with the punctual understanding of choice,[18] virtue is narrative: it has length. The present is embedded in a past which has made me who I am and reaches toward a hope which is already present to faith. Virtue as well has breadth: it is communal. My decision has neighbors, persons who count on me, persons far and near, and groups, with whom I am bound by reciprocal promises and role expectations. Virtue also has depth: it implies and celebrates understandings about the nature of person, the nature of God, the goodness and fallenness of creation, the inwardness and the transparency of self, the miracles of redemptive transformation. . . .

The Underlying Axiom

We should then not be surprised if within this newly retrieved traditional format there would be concern for war and peace. In fact, there turns out to be less than one might have expected;[19] yet one prominent example exists: *The Peaceable Kingdom*, by Stanley Hauerwas.[20] The rejection of war is not derived from a pragmatic calculation nor from a principled deduction. Instead, it comes from being the kind of humans for whom violence against their neighbors cannot even arise as a possible choice.

A *Shortcoming*

The rhetoric of virtue, however, uses terms that are old and fuzzy. They do not foster crisp distinctions as do the other ethical game rules about prescribed ends or proscribed means. Where does patience end and peaceableness begin?[21] Is meekness a virtue or a vice?[22] Is there one kind of love or two or three?[23] Are there seven virtues or twelve?[24] Can they be clearly defined?

It is not always clear that moving away from picking crucial decisions apart will enable us after the reorientation to resolve those decisions more adequately. Some fear that it is rather merely evading the hard choices. Not all of those who argue that the language of virtue is the best language for ethical discourse then go on to prove the point by describing the moral life in a more clear and binding way.

Nevertheless

Yet the language of virtue and vice[25] can restore a salutary wholeness to the vision of the moral life. It frees the person who renounces violence from the constraint of proving for every possible case, consequentially, that the best possible outcome will result. It frees from scrupulosity about cases in favor of cultivating the kind of character which makes decisions easier. It frees from individualism because the stories which exemplify our commitment, the telling of which reinforces our training in virtue, are shared.

After All

The military life has always been described in virtue terms. The ideal soldier is seldom described as one who incisively makes hard decisions according to all the rules and all the facts. He is rather the person marked by temperance, courage, justice, prudence. The honors and promotions he receives are determined more by his showing those qualities than by his solving all his problems cleanly.

19

The Pacifism of the Messianic Community

The hint half guessed, the gift half understood,
is Incarnation.
  —T. S. Eliot

It is not by accident that the writer of 1 Peter said that Jesus carried men's sins "in his own body." Because it happened in Jesus' body, it can also happen in ours.
  —Walter Klaassen, *What Have You to Do with Peace?*

The more carefully and respectfully I have sought to interpret the positions of others, the more difficult it becomes for me not to make my own view benefit unfairly from comparisons. The critical observer can of course discern in this last position as well a combination of several distinct strands, which might be further dissected.[1]

To say that this is the pacifism of the *messianic* community is to affirm its dependence upon the confession that Jesus is Christ and that Jesus Christ is Lord. To say that Jesus is the Messiah is to say that in him are fulfilled the expectations of God's people regarding the coming one in whom God's will would perfectly be done. Therefore, in the person and work of Jesus, in his teachings and his passion, this kind of pacifism finds its rootage, and in his resurrection it finds its enablement.

When we confess Jesus as Messiah, we find his uniqueness and his authority not simply in his religious teachings or in his spiritual depth. His authority is expressed also in the way he went about representing a new moral option in Palestine, at the cost of his death.

The Underlying Axiom

It follows that the character of such a messianic-community position can be known only in relation to Jesus Christ. This simple sentence is not as obvious as it may at first seem. It is a statement first of all about the nature of revelation. On our own resources, we cannot possibly figure out just what it means to believe in Jesus as Christ, or just what it means to follow Jesus Christ as revealer of the nature and will of God. This position is thus comparable to the principled (type 3) and the cultic (13) positions described above. It makes its appeal clearly to something that people must be told.

Yet it varies from those two types decisively. The telling has come to us not on a tablet of stone chiseled by the finger of God alone on Sinai, or from the mouth of a prophet or an oracle. Instead, the telling has come in the full humanity of a unique and yet complete human being. Note well that although all of the positions reviewed above are held by Christians, this is the only position for which the person of Jesus is indispensable. It is the only one of these positions which would lose its substance if Jesus were not Christ and would lose its foundation if Jesus Christ were not Lord.

Since Jesus is seen in his full humanity as responding to needs and temptations of a social character, the problems of our obedience to him are not problems in the interpretation of texts. Nor is the question of our fidelity to him one of moralism, a stuffy preoccupation with never making a mistake. The question put to us as we follow Jesus is not whether we have successfully refrained from breaking any rules. Instead, we are asked whether we have been participants in that human experience, that peculiar way of living for God in the world and being used as instruments of the living of God in the world,[2] which the Bible calls *agapē* or cross.

When we speak of the pacifism of the messianic *community,* we move the focus of ethical concern from the individual to the human community experiencing in its shared life a foretaste of God's kingdom. Persons may severally and separately ask themselves about right and wrong in their concern for their own integrity. That is fine as far as it goes. The messianic community's experience, however, is different in that it is not a life alone for heroic personalities. Instead, it is a life for a society. It is communal in that it is lived by a covenanting group of men and women who instruct one another, forgive one another, bear one another's burdens, and reinforce one another's witness.

Think back over the line of varieties of religious pacifism. We could have pointed out along the way that the major streams of pacifist experience (except for the particularly withdrawn communal ones, types of chapters 9, 14-15) tend to be represented by powerful individuals. These persons have perhaps numerous sympathizers but few followers, no congregation, and only limited success in creating a movement.

This community resource is not merely a moral crutch or a psychological springboard which enables individuals to feel more free and confident as they take pacifist positions. Even that would be nothing to sneeze at. Being crippled, I am unashamed of needing a crutch; and most of us are moral cripples. Yet the social meaning of a peace witness is far more fundamental than that. The existence of a human community dedicated in common to a new and publicly scandalous enemy-loving way of life is itself a new social datum. A heroic individual can crystallize a widespread awareness of need or widespread admiration. However, only a continuing community dedicated to a deviant value system can change the world.

A Shortcomings

When measured by the standards of the critical ethicist, this view suffers because it is not for all people. Those who uphold it affirm that the discipleship of which they speak is a necessary reflection of the true meaning of Jesus. The call to follow Jesus is a call addressed to all people. But the standards by which such a life is guided are not cut to the measure of persons in general. That pattern of life can be clearly perceived—to say nothing of being even modestly and partially lived—only through that reorientation of the personality and its expression which Jesus and his first followers called repentance and new birth.

Repentance initiates that authentic human existence to which all are called. But as long as a given person or a given society has not undergone that change of direction, it is not meaningful to describe how they would live as pacifists. Thus it is not possible to extrapolate directly from this stance of faith a strategy for resolving the urban crisis or the arms race of the crisis in the Middle East tomorrow. This position can not be institutionalized to work just as well among those who do not quite understand it or are not sure how much they believe in it.[3]

Many count it a further disadvantage that this position is utterly dependent upon who Jesus was and the attitude one takes toward him. All of the positions mentioned above call for some kind of commitment and some kind of "faith." All of them are minority positions which can be taken only by someone willing to run risks and be different.

However, as we have seen, *only this* messianic-community position collapses if Jesus be not Christ or if Jesus Christ be not Lord. This is a disadvantage for some kinds of Christians, and for others it is not. It is a serious drawback for most habits of ethical deliberation. Christian theologians are generally dedicated to making Jesus normative in their thought about deity and the creeds. Yet many of them tend to be startled by the suggestion that Jesus might be indispensable in defining a proper political humanity.

Another disadvantage of this position is that it does not promise to "work." It cannot promise "success" as, for example, programmatic pacifism (type 4) can do to a modest degree. We cannot sight down the barrel of suffering love to see how it will hit its target. The resurrection is not the end product of a mechanism which runs through its paces wherever there is a crucifixion. The Christian hope in the kingdom embraces that peculiar kind of hoping assurance which is called faith. But this is not the preponderant probability of early success which is desired by the just-war theory or by a prudential ethic.

Nevertheless

This position is closer than the others to the idiom of the Bible and to the core affirmations of the Christian faith. It reckons seriously with the hopelessness of the world as it stands and yet affirms a gospel of hope. It shares the integrity of the principled views (types 3, 8-9, 14) without their withdrawal from history. It includes the practical concern of the programmatic views (types 2, 4-5) without placing its hope there.

After All

The invocation of violence to support any cause is also implicitly a messianism. Any national sense of mission claims implicitly to be a saving community. One cannot avoid either messianism or the claim to chosen peoplehood by setting Jesus or his methods aside. One only casts the aura of election around lesser causes.

20

What Have We Learned?

Careful reflection upon this variety of patterns of thought may throw some light on our conversation about Christian faithfulness today.

Examining Prior Assumptions

It is easy to distort the discussion about the Christian and war by transmuting it into a comparison of ethical systems. As we moved through the inventory above, the critical reader has noticed that in most cases the models of ethical thought with which we were dealing represented attitudes not simply to war but to the whole problem of ethics. Arguments of almost the same form could have been presented section by section for dealing with monogamy, promise-keeping, truth-telling, or art.

Since post-Niebuhrian nonpacifists reject pacifism, they see all pacifism as utopian purism (types 8-9) or as withdrawal (9, 13-16), rather than recognizing a respectable pacifist argument when presented in their own terms (2 or 4). The advocates of situation ethics reject pacifism for its inflexible principles (3, 8). They do not bother to take seriously those pacifisms which calculate carefully in the situation (2), or which preserve the integrity of the loving disposition of free decision in every context (11).

In such cases, in other words, people are not really discussing war; they are talking past each other out of logically incompatible prior assumptions about whether and how one can think morally at all. Each kind of pacifist position has its rootage in a wider context and should be fairly evaluated only in that frame of reference.

Comparing Logics

The argument around pacifism is only one of the points where the multiplicity of our models of ethical thought becomes manifest. Academic Protestant ethical thought in midcentury was largely dominated by the social-responsibility models of the brothers H. Richard and Reinhold Niebuhr. Academic Catholic thought was comparably dominated by older principle-application models, and by the changes in those patterns arising out of internal self-criticism.

New approaches to the problem of war played only a small role in those developments. That has begun to change in both families, and there have been rapprochements and overlappings among the several denominational worlds (including the evangelicals and the philosophers, not mentioned above) which cannot be reviewed here. Only for a few of these developments has the issue of war been part of the picture.

Does not the manifold diversity of the approaches displayed above call us to a less monochromatic practice of ethical theologizing? Each of these logics has its own integrity, as we noted under the regular rubric "Nevertheless." In each case we were able to criticize but not really to refute. Must we seek to boil each type of pacifism down to where we can call it an inferior version of some other approach?

Weaving Threads Together

My first plea is thus that each type of pacifist reasoning be respected in its own right. From that, it should not be inferred that a position which holds purely to one of these "types" will be more worthy of respect, or more effective, than one which blends them. I admit that *in some cases* mixing the modes may make for serious moral or practical confusion, especially when pragmatic arguments (type 4) or just-war reasoning (2) are interlocked with some of the others.[1]

Nevertheless, it may well be the case that a position which weaves together more than one compatible strand will be more convincing, more effective, and more viable. Examples might be the positions of Martin Luther King, Jr. (types 4-5, 7, and perhaps 3), of the Catholic Worker (1, 3, 6, 9), and of Anabaptism (3, 9, 14-15). Here are fabrics where the several threads reinforce one another.

Recognizing Practical Common Conviction

A final in-group word might be addressed to the attitude of those ethically dualistic Mennonites (type 16) who, by eschewing "pacifism," risk an unavowed and uncritical acquiescence in nationalism. Their critical point is well taken. There are many kinds of pacifism held to by many kinds of Christians for many kinds of reasons (to say nothing of several more non-Christian types which we have only hinted at here). They should not be confused with each other.

Yet, having recognized this, it is time for nonresistant Mennonites to move beyond their initial defensive reflex to the recognition of a real degree of practical common conviction. They do and properly should share this common persuasion with non-Christian pacifists and (much more) with non-Mennonite Christian pacifists. There is not and need not be total agreement. But at every point a shared antiwar commitment *nevertheless* represents a greater degree of commonality and a clearer recognition of common adversaries than when Mennonites are so concerned to stand clear of pacifism that they unconsciously but practically become covert militarists.

There is certainly a real sense in which Christians in any country, and therefore also Mennonite Christians in the United States, are not simply Americans like all their neighbors. Nevertheless, it would be more nearly correct, and contribute more logically to reasonable discussion, to say that they are Americans of a particular kind. They are Mennonite Christian Americans, not denying their origins and identity and pretending to be Russian or Argentine or Vietcong.

Likewise, there are ways Mennonites can contribute more to sober conversation. They can stop fixing upon an irrational avoidance of the word "pacifist." Instead, they can recognize with more precision and responsibility, more ecumenically and supportively, the varieties of ways in which people are led to recognize the wrongness of war and to devote themselves to the service of their fellow human beings.

Sometimes these fellow pacifists come to their positions by intelligent analysis, sometimes by emotional revulsion, sometimes by irrational optimism, and sometimes perhaps by the Spirit of God (whose workings may not always be completely distinguishable from "all of the above"). They may arrive at pacifism in ways or under labels and with understandings other than those a historic peace church has found most adequate. Yet they merit and may need recognition from and dialogue with the peace church communions. The christological nonresistance of the Radical Reformation or of the Historic Peace Churches is *nevertheless* one form of Christian pacifism, and it is most honest when it is ready to be counted as such.

Seeing the Critique Boomerang, *After All*

I have reviewed an assortment of varieties of religious pacifism. Now we need to reflect on the whole. It can be argued cogently that any ethical system, if taken seriously and as more than self-justification, can lead to one kind of pacifism or another. Indeed, it can cogently be demonstrated that some ethical systems *must* lead to pacifism.

These various pacifisms are sometimes compatible with one another, sometimes even mutually reinforcing (13-16; or 1-2, 4), and sometimes directly contradictory in their assumptions (4 versus 8-9, 16). Yet they are no more so than are the varied reasons people have for participating in war. In their denunciation of war, however it be explained, the moral commonality of all of them is greater than the systematic diversity.

We therefore can and should direct one form or another of the pacifist appeal to every ethical system, to every morally responsible stance a Christian can take. *As indicated under the rubric "After All," every serious critique one can address to the pacifist, if taken honestly, turns back with greater force upon the advocate of war.*

Appendix 1

Speaking Truth to Power: Quaker Political Witness

Although as a denominational fellowship, Friends in America are few in number, and as diverse as any other small denomination—perhaps more so—there still exists an impressive record of peacemaking initiatives carried out on the basis of the special Quaker vision of things. It refutes the easy assumption of the uninformed that pacifists are out of touch with practicality.

There is a specific Quaker way to deal with social and political issues, taking sensitive and serious account of the political facts. The Quakers contributed to opening contacts with the Soviet Union forty years ago, seeking new options in the debate about the Middle East, debating about atomic armament....

Those Quaker messages, search processes, and ongoing analysis on specific major world political issues—they do not originate from simple Christian humanist optimism. They are serious social science studies. One may disagree with their reading of the facts or disagree with their theology, but they are both theologically coherent and scientific in their intention, if you study their data. The authors of these studies are not utopian visionaries. The theology which enabled William Penn three centuries ago to try to make something of his unique opportunity for a political fresh start as head of a colony is still a theology which orients people in serious social involvement.

The modern incarnation of the traditional Quaker vision for concrete peacemaking is especially well represented by a series of brief studies which have been circulated quite widely in the time since World War II. The following chronological list is representative, not complete:

Quaker Studies

The United States and the Soviet Union: Some Quaker Proposals for Peace. New Haven: Yale University Press, 1949.

Steps to Peace: A Quaker View of U.S. Foreign Policy. Philadelphia: American Friends Service Committee (AFSC), 1951.

Speak Truth to Power: A Quaker Search for an Alternative to Violence, A Study of International Conflict. AFSC, 1955.

"Is There Another Way? A Memorable Debate. . . ." A response to *Speak Truth to Power*, in *Progressive*, Oct. 1955.

A New China Policy: Some Quaker Proposals. New Haven: Yale University Press, 1965.

Peace in Vietnam. New York: Hill and Wang, 1965.

In Place of War: An Inquiry into Nonviolent National Defense. New York: Grossman Pubs., 1967.

Search for Peace in the Middle East. New York: Fawcett, 1970.

Toward Middle East Dialogue: Responses to the Quakers' Report. Committee on New Alternatives, 1972.

A Compassionate Peace: A Future for the Middle East. New York: Hill and Wang, 1982; updated 1989.

South Africa: Challenge and Hope. Lyle Tatum, ed. New York: Hill and Wang, 2d ed., 1987.

Two Koreas—One Future? John Sullivan and Roberta Foss, eds. AFSC; Lanham, Md.: University Press of America, 1987.

Breaking with a Bitter Past: Toward a New U.S. Relationship with Central America. AFSC, 1987.

Quaker Process and Dialogue

The point of this present note is not to digest the specific content of any one of these studies, but to characterize the series as a whole, as characteristic of the specific kind of pacifism behind it:

1. The Quakers identify their witness with their heritage; they use "Quaker" unapologetically as an adjective to label what they are doing, representing a prototypical, understandable, respectable stance. They are not apologetic about it, as Mennonites might be, nor do they, like some recent Catholic thinkers, promise without checking with the others that all "people of good will" could do the same—though that might be true.

2. The reports are the result of committee dialogue, and usually of substantial field study, providing for conversation with people on all sides of the questions studied.

3. Although illuminated by Quaker convictions about human dignity, conflict and peace-making, the fact-finding process and the analysis are done in terms intended to make sense to anyone of good will, and are generally successful in being so understood. They usually find publishers and readers.

4. This acceptance of the language of "the others" or of "the authorities" includes a theologically conscious adjustment to the awareness that one cannot directly impose gospel language and values on the wider world; yet the Quakers refuse to grant that that recognition cuts them off from speaking. The title given to one of their texts, "Speak Truth to Power," expresses that confidence. This is thought to be a classical phrase from early Quakerism.

5. The process is dictated by the conviction that both (or all) sides of a tense situation not only need to be heard, but have a right to have their concerns taken account of in any situation. This is the operational import of the old Quaker phrase, "speaking to that of God in every man."

6. The process is dictated by the conviction that fact-based dialogue, involving the interested parties, however

painful, is more likely to produce results that are to some degree just, than solutions imposed by superior power or by destruction. Precisely because the results are more just and fair, they will probably be to some degree more durable.

7. The way of carrying out these reconciling conversations is not the subject of any "how to do it" manual or any training course. There is no bookshelf of literature about how it works. What is listed below is not from the center of the movement. Quakers seem to acquire this style or skill by osmosis, not by formal training.

8. The proposals are concrete and realistic; one even mentioned "steps" in its title.

9. Most of the reports are successful in provoking serious dialogue well beyond the borders of the religious community. Most of the texts find commercial publishers. Several see more than one edition. Several provoke follow-up publications (listed above in two cases).

10. The timing of these initiatives is regularly well ahead of the readiness of the wider public to face the same issues. Especially with regard to the Soviet Union and China, directions for major policy changes were charted which years later were found feasible by people in power.

11. There is no embarrassment about running the risks of being "too objective" for some critics and "not objective enough" for others.

The entire corpus would be worthy of study as a phenomenon in the field of political science as well as of Christian ethics. Though Quakers are convinced that under God this kind of work is a good thing to do, they evidence little interest in praising God by narrating or analyzing it. Not only are Friends relatively uninterested in recounting their good works. Several of the Quakers I consulted in the process of preparing the above summary were disinclined to take any credit for the originality of the formal qualities just noted.

This summary of one dominant and nearly unique type of Quaker "witness" leaves aside several other categories of peacemaking which are not less significant, but may be characteristic, formally not unique to Quakers, though led by them:

Studies Led by Quaker Individuals

These sample studies are committed to the same kind of truth-based, dialogical problem-solving, but are not produced by a group:

Ron Young. *Missed Opportunities for Peace: U.S. Middle East Policy 1981-1986.* Philadelphia: AFSC, 1987.

John Lamperti. *What Are We Afraid Of? An Assessment of the "Communist Threat" in Central America.* Boston: South End Press, 1988.

Philip Berryman: Various papers and books on Central America.

Studies by Quaker Groups

There are other studies on domestic political matters and strategies for profound social change done by particular Quaker clusters. For example, we note the publications of the Movement for a New Society, which grew out of "A Quaker Action Group."

Quaker Peacemaking Action

The Quakers are engaging in mediation and conciliation activities which actually bring the conflicting parties together. Samples are found in the following:

C. H. Mike Yarrow. *Quaker Experiences in International Conciliation.* New Haven: Yale University Press, 1978.

Paul Wehr. *Conflict Regulation.* Boulder: Westview Press, 1979.

Joseph B. Stuhlberg. *Taking Charge: Managing Conflict.* Lexington: Heath, 1987.

Quaker Preparation for Mediation

Quakers are also known for their premediation activities fostering acquaintance and trust among diplomatic personnel, as shown in the following:

Landrum Bolling. "Quaker Work in the Middle East," pp. 80ff., in *Unofficial Diplomats*. Maureen R. Berman and Joseph E. Johnson, eds. New York: Columbia University Press, 1977.

Adam Curle. *In the Middle: Non-Official Mediation in Violent Situations*. New York: St. Martin's Press.

Cynthia Sampson. *A Study of the International Conciliation Work of Religious Figures*. Harvard Law School, Program on Negotiation.

Appendix 2

The Spectrum of Nonpacifist Postures

The background of our effort to be fair to "pacifism" in all its varieties should properly be joined with a similar concern to disentangle from one another the several (quite different) ways to be nonpacifist. We will not take the space here to review the intellectual history of how these clarifications have arisen. It should suffice for the reader's general orientation that I lay out the list as simply as possible, in the order of ascending distance from "pacifism."

A. *The Just-War Tradition*

The just-war tradition (JWT), properly so-called, provides for a considerable number of objective criteria to be applied to a particular case. The purpose is to determine whether that given war is (as is true most of the time) wrong or (in some cases which meet the requirements) justified. As we saw above (chapter 2), when the answer in a given case is negative, when the war is not justified, this position agrees (in practice) with the pacifist, and is sometimes called pacifism.

B. *Toothless Just-War Talk*

It is also possible to use the language of the just-war tradition but without seriously contemplating hard choices which might arise. This may be because one has no concept of the possible use of JWT language to say no to a war. It may be because one believes on philosophical grounds[1] that there can be no common criteria between pacifists and nonpacifists. We might call this a "toothless" version of the JWT. In reality, decisions are made on the basis of some other understanding farther down on this list. The "justice" language is used in advocacy of war but not in restraint.

C. Governmental Self-Interest

There is the view that it is not possible to apply moral criteria to government, since by the nature of the case a sovereign government is accountable to no authority and no values above the preservation of its own power. This is currently most often called "realism."[2] In ancient Greece it was held by people called Cynics and in Renaissance Italy it was exposited by Machiavelli.[3] Clausewitz restated it in terms of the soldier's profession.[4] This view involves two kinds of logical difficulty:

1. It is often laid out by people[5] who say that to apply moral thought to war is *wrong*. Yet there is a moral obligation after all in this area, since the state's unaccountable self-interest is not an intractable, undiscussible surd but is supposed to have a positive value. It is morally right, they say, to argue that moral language should not be used, and to act in ways which moral language condemns.

2. It is assumed without discussion that "national interest" is clearly defined. But is it the interest of the ruling class? of "the people"? Does that "interest" include self-respect and promise-keeping?

Nevertheless, there are those who with conviction make the claim that restraint on the basis of any other consideration than enlightened self-interest should not be asked of governments.

D. Holy War

There is the view that war is a holy cause since God (any god) has called for it. Examples are the ancient Hebrew war of YHWH (Yahweh, the LORD), the medieval European crusades, the Islamic jihad, or for that matter the fascist cause. All these are morally mandatory not on just-war grounds related to particular cases, but because one army considers itself divinely called to destroy God's enemies.

Thus in World War I the Germans claimed *Gott mit uns* (God with us), and on the other side, a typical American preacher proclaimed, "It is God who has summoned us to this war. It is his war we are fighting. . . . This crusade is indeed a crusade. The greatest in history—the holiest . . . a Holy War. Yes, it is Christ, the King of Righteousness, who calls us to grapple in deadly strife with this unholy and blasphemous power [Germany]."[6]

E. Rambo

There is the view that war is made imperative for a particular man because thereby he acts out (or achieves) his manhood. People on the other side of the clash have no status; they are the fodder for his proving his own dignity to himself. Our word for this is "Rambo"; it used to be John Wayne.[7]

Beyond these five basic types, there remain two other ways of evaluating war which at first may seem to be different:

• Supreme Emergency

Michael Walzer[8] has added to the picture the notion of "supreme emergency," when it would be justified to break the ordinary JWT rules because all of civilization is at stake. This is really part of the JWT reasoning process, with a weak spot leaning toward the "toothless" variant.

That it is still in that family is demonstrated by the fact that the exception needs to be justified by an extreme threat, and further by Walzer's saying that the infraction must not be glorified. The general who is responsible for those war crimes, though the crimes were indispensable, must not be decorated.

• *War Is Hell*

General Sherman gave currency to the phrase "war is hell" to designate the fact that his march through Georgia did not recognize the rules of fair fighting. In his case the argument was that making the enemy people suffer more will make them surrender sooner.[9] Others who use the argument mean that once a war has begun, there is no one who can make a responsible decision to keep it from taking its course.[10] The argument is deceptive, however; believing war to be "hell," one could always stay home and let it take its course. One could even sue for peace. The reason that after having called it "hell" one keeps on fighting, responsibly and vigorously pursuing its course across the land, still needs to come from one of the above considerations (A-E) or some mixture thereof.

The Logics of Nonpacifism

Thus, recognizing that the "Supreme Emergency" and "War Is Hell" views really depend on other reasons, there do seem to be only five types of nonpacifist postures. These five modes of moral discourse are fundamentally different in their logic, even though the terminology of the JWT will often be used by persons who at bottom reason in one of the other ways.

The pacifist will agree, most of the time, with the authentic just-war thinker (type A): whenever the criteria are honestly used, most wars will not be acceptable. Even when a war's arising drives them apart, the pacifist and the just-war thinker will agree (against the other four positions, B-E) to oppose the loss of all restraint.

On the other hand, the pacifist will sometimes agree with the other positions about the facts of the case: The pacifist and the realist (C) both doubt whether it is possible to transcend selfishness and exercise moral and legal restraint and still have a chance to win the war. The pacifist and the crusader (D) agree to doubt whether a population once mobilized will be patient with the disciplines of fighting fair, and they agree that political decisions are not derived from pragmatic calculations.

Nevertheless

Yet we shall understand the debate more adequately if we separate the different kinds of nonpacifist moral reasoning from one another.

Appendix 3

Nonviolent National Defense Alternatives

In the first edition of *Nevertheless*, I already referred to the existence of a body of research and planning literature on how to defend one's national values without war, and that note has been retained (see note 6 to chapter 4). The following listing is incomplete but should suffice to demonstrate the relevance of the search for alternatives to violence, not only on other levels of society but also in the defense of national values. Sometimes the term used is "Civilian-Based Defense," sometimes "transarmament." The sources listed were selected to accentuate the variety of orientations and the fact that this field of research is by no means brand new.

Selected Sources on Nonviolent Defense

American Friends Service Committee. *In Place of War: An Inquiry into Non-Violent National Defense*. New York: Grossman, 1962.

Atheston, Edward B. "The Relevance of Civilian-Based Defense to U.S. Security Interests," in *The Military Review*, May 1976:24ff., and June 1976:45ff.

Baez, Joan. "Personal Commitment to Nonviolent Social Change," (a 1970 *Playboy* interview) in Israel W. Charny, *Strategies Against Violence: Design for Nonviolent Change*. Boulder: Westview Press, 1978:116ff.

Boserup, Anders, and Andrew Mack. *War Without Weapons: Non-Violence in National Defense.* New York: Schocken, 1975.

Bruyn, Severyn. "Social Theory of Nonviolent Action: A Framework for Research in Creative Conflict," in Severyn T. Bruyn and Paula Rayman, eds., *Nonviolent Action and Social Change.* New York: Halstead Press, 1979:13ff.

David, Randolf S. "The Theory and Practice of Unarmed Resistance," in *Third World Studies,* Special Issues Series, 6. Manila: Third World Studies Centre, College of Social Science and Philosophy, University of the Philippines, 1985.

Deutsch, Morton. *The Resolution of Conflict.* New Haven: Yale University Press, 1973 (esp. pp. 400ff.).

Freund, Norman C. *Nonviolent National Defense.* New York: University Press of America, 1987.

Geeraerts, Gustaaf, ed. *Possibilities of Civilian Defense in Western Europe.* Amsterdam: Swets & Zeitlinger, 1977.

Gregg, Richard B. *The Power of Non-Violence.* Philadelphia: Lippincott, 1934.

––––––––––––––––. *Training for Peace.* Philadelphia: Lippincott, 1931.

Hare, A. Paul, and Herbert H. Blumberg, eds. *Liberation Without Violence: A Third Party Approach.* Lanham, Md.: Rowman and Littlefield, 1978.

Harman, Smoke. *Paths to Peace.* Boulder: Westview Press, 1987.

Hughan, Jessie Wallace, and Cecil Hinshaw. "Toward a Non-Violent National Defense," in Mulford K. Sibley, *The Quiet Battle.* New York: Doubleday/Anchor, 1963:316ff.

Irwin, Bob. *U.S. Defense Policy: Mainstream Views and Nonviolent Alternatives.* Waltham, Mass.: Institute for Nonviolent Action, 1982.

King-Hall, Stephen. *Defense in a Nuclear Age.* Nyack, N.Y.: Fellowship of Reconciliation, 1959.

Lakey, George. "Sociological Mechanisms of Nonviolence," in Rayman Bruyn, ed., *Nonviolent Action and Social Change.* New York: Irvington Publishers, 1979:64ff.

Moulton, Phillips P. *Violence, or Aggressive Nonviolent Resistance?* Pendle Hill Pamphlets, 178. Wallingford, Pa.: Pendle Hill Pubns., 1971.

Norman, Liane Ellison. "Non-Violent Defined," in Ronald H. Stone and Dana W. Wilbanks, eds., *Peacemaking Struggle: Militarism and Resistance.* Presbyterian Church, USA; Lanham, Md.: University Press of America, 1985:263-274.

Roberts, Adam, ed. *Civilian Resistance as National Defense.* Baltimore:

Penguin, 1969. Also published as *The Strategy of Civilian Defense.* London: Faber & Faber, 1970.

Schell, Jonathan. "The Choice," in Donna Gregory, ed. *The Nuclear Predicament.* New York: St. Martin's Press, 1986:310ff.

Seifert, Harvey. *Conquest by Suffering.* Philadelphia: Westminster, 1965.

Sharp, Gene. *Exploring Nonviolent Alternatives.* Boston: Porter Sargent, 1970.

_____. *Making the Abolition of War a Realistic Goal.* New York: Institute for World Order, 1980.

_____. *Making Europe Unconquerable: A Civilian-Based Deterrence and Defense System.* London: Taylor/Francis, 1985; and Cambridge, U.K.: Bellinger, 1986.

_____. *National Security Through Civilian-Based Defense.* Omaha: Association for Transarmament Studies, 1985.

_____. *The Politics of Nonviolent Action.* Boston: Porter Sargent, 1973.

_____. *Social Power and Political Freedom.* Boston: Porter Sargent, 1989.

Shridharani, Krishnalal Jethalal. *War Without Violence.* New York: Harcourt Brace, 1939.

Sider, Ronald J., and Richard K. Taylor. "Fighting Fire with Water," in *Sojourners,* April 1983; and in *Nuclear Holocaust and Christian Hope.* Downers Grove: InterVarsity Press, 1982; also at Mahwah, N.J.: Paulist Press, 1983.

_____. "International Aggression and Non-Military Defense," in *The Christian Century,* July 6-13, 1983:643-47.

_____. *Non-Violence: The Invincible Weapon?* Waco, Tex.: Word Books, 1989.

_____. *Nuclear Holocaust and Christian Hope.* Downers Grove: InterVarsity Press, 1982 (esp. pp. 231-294).

Wehr, Paul. "Nonviolent Resistance to Occupation: Norway and Czechoslovakia," in Rayman Bruyn, ed., *Nonviolent Action and Social Change.* New York: Irvington Publishers, 1979:213ff.

Woito, Robert. *To End War: A New Approach to International Conflict.* 6th ed. New York: Pilgrim Press, 1982 (esp. pp. 89-195).

The Thin Blue Line

When the United Nations assigns a group of soldiers to patrol a truce line or in some other way to keep the peace and they possess arms but are forbidden to use them, this is more like nonviolent action than like war.

Higgins, Rosalyn, and Michael Harbottle. "United Nations Peacekeeping; Past Lessons and Future Prospects" (memorial lecture). London: David Davies Memorial Institute of International Studies, 1971.

Keyes, Gene. "Peacekeeping by Unarmed Buffer Forces: Precedents and Proposals," in *Peace and Change* 5 (nos. 2-3, Fall 1978): 3-10.

Rikhye, Indar, Michael Harbottle, and Bjorn Egge. *The Thin Blue Line: International Peacekeeping and Its Future.* New Haven: Yale University Press, 1974.

United Nations Staff. *The Blue Helmets: A Review of United Nations Peace-Keeping.* 2d ed. New York: United Nations, 1990.

Notes

Preface

1. This is especially the case when those speaking for the same position can sometimes accept and sometimes reject the same label. Chapter 16 (below) demonstrates that such is the case in at least one tradition.

2. It would be a fascinating exercise to cross-reference all the logical types here described with the texts gathered in the two best anthologies on the subject: Peter Mayer's *The Pacifist Conscience* (Chicago: Henry Regnery Co., 1967), and Arthur and Lila Weinbergs, eds., *Instead of Violence* (Boston: Beacon Press, 1965). I shall not attempt this. The degree of complexity and coverage already attained is sufficient to make the point of this essay. I shall note parallels to the major strands lifted up in Geoffrey Nuttall's *Christian Pacifism in History* (Oxford: Blackwell, 1958). Another challenging survey of types is offered by John Richard Burkholder and Barbara Nelson Gingerich, *Mennonite Peace Theology: A Panorama of Types* (Akron Pa.: Mennonite Central Committee, 1991).

3. A papal message of December 1967 said, "The word peace does not mean pacifism, it does not hide a cowardly and lazy conception of life. . . ." Again in 1991 John Paul II said, "We are not pacifists. We don't want peace at any cost." This slurring apposition between pacifism and moral weakness is perhaps more excusable in view of the word's usage in the European languages, for which *appeasement* would probably be a better translation than the literal equivalent *pacifism*. It is not focused upon the practice of conscientious objection. It refers to the projection, not necessarily for idealistic reasons, of a nonmilitant policy for a nation.

1. The Pacifism of Christian Cosmopolitanism

1. *Pacem in Terris*, April 11 (Holy Thursday), 1963. Although the text makes no reference to its immediate provocation, the appearance of this encyclical, after the Vatican Council had begun its deliberations and just a few months before the death of John XXIII, testifies to the special pastoral concern provoked in his mind by the Cuban missile crisis. (Since Roman Catholic documents are widely available in numerous editions, no specific sources are cited here or below.)

2. "If you want to be brothers, let the weapons fall from your hands," said Paul VI to the General Assembly of the United Nations on October 4, 1965. Since then, this concern became still more widely evident in the work of the second Vatican Council (*Gaudium et Spes: The Church in the Modern World*, especially chapter V). Since then its expression has tended to take the form described in chapter 2 of this book.

3. Cf. pp. 110-112 in Roland Bainton, *Christian Attitudes to War and Peace* (Nashville: Abingdon, 1961); cf. also the index references to "truce" and "peace of God" in James T. Johnson, *The Quest for Peace* (Princeton, N.J.: Princeton University Press, 1987).

4. Benedict XV, who was pope during World War I, regularly condemned war and called for peace. Some of his statements are gathered in Harry W. Flannery, ed., *Pattern for Peace* (Newman Press, 1962), pp. 9ff. It had no effect upon the Roman Catholics in either Germany or France, whose cardinals (on both sides) continued to rule that this time war was justified.

Thus a propaganda pamphlet, *La Guerre Allemande et le Catholicisme*, was published under the editorial direction of the rector of the *Institut Catholique* of Paris with a preface by the Cardinal Archbishop of Paris, proving that the French cause was just. Within a few months the response of German Catholics was printed: *Der deutsche Krieg und der Katholizmus; Deutsche Abwehr franzoesische Angriffe*, with a German cardinal's telegram as frontispiece.

By noting this religious provincialism, I do not suggest that Protestant provincialism is morally any less reprehensible. But at least Protestants do not claim to be one visible ecclesiastical communion and then deny that claim in practice.

5. An example of this weakness is evident in the reproaches which have since been cast on the memory of Pius XII. Some judge that, by not roundly and publicly condemning Nazi genocide, he failed adequately to risk his pastoral status.

2. The Pacifism of the Honest Study of Cases

1. I have offered a simple description of this position in my *When War Is Unjust* (Minneapolis: Augsburg Press, 1984). An early general introduction to just-war thought was *War and Moral Discourse*, by Ralph Potter (Atlanta: John Knox Press, 1969). The fullest contemporary coverage of the theme is in the many writings of Paul Ramsey and James T. Johnson.

2. Although the nature of nuclear war was known in principle since 1945, it was not until the mid-1950s that important Christian moral thinkers began spelling out what that meant in just-war terms: cf. Thomas Taylor and Robert S. Bilheimer, *Christians and the Prevention of War in an Atomic Age: A Theological Discussion* (London: SCM Press, 1961). This booklet reports on an ecumenical discussion group whose work was done in 1957. Similar positions were taken at about the same time by the Protestant Paul Ramsey, by the Catholic John Courtney Murray, S.J., and in Germany by the *Kirchliche Bruderschaften*.

3. *The Divine Imperative* (ET 1936) is here quoted from the 1947 edition (Philadelphia: Westminster), pp. 469-474.

4. The high point of Roman Catholic responsibility in this realm was the promulgation in 1983 of the pastoral letter *The Challenge of Peace*, making a firm statement that the current nuclear policies of the USA were morally unacceptable. This event may be considered as combining the postures here described separately in chapters 1 and 2.

5. I use here the word *doctrine* because it is habitual; yet the noun *tradition* would be more accurate; *doctrine* seems to suggest more simplicity and unanimity than really exists. I shall abbreviate *just-war tradition* as JWT to designate the tradition.

6. A now-familiar case in point is the misunderstanding of Karl Barth's near-pacifist position. See my *Karl Barth and the Problem of War* (Nashville: Abingdon Press, 1970), pp. 73, 103-105.

7. The term *unjust-war objector*, though clumsy, may be the most precise. It is suggested by Charles Lutz, as noted in my book *When War Is Unjust*, pp. 7ff. Also see Lutz, "Objection to Participation in Combat: Legality and Morality," in Paul Peachey (ed.), *Peace, Politics, and the People of God* (Philadelphia: Fortress Press, 1986), pp. 151-162.

The more current term *selective objector* first came into current use in the late 1960s. It accentuates what distinguishes one kind of conscientious objector from others rather than what stands at the center of one's own position. It wrongly suggests that the selectiveness may be whimsical or irresponsible; instead, the selective objector intends to be responsible. The logic and respectability of its claims were given formal recognition in 1968 by the World Council of Churches and by Catholic and Lutheran bodies in the USA. Cf. James Finn, *A Conflict of Loyalties: The Case for Selective Objection* (New York: Pegasus, 1969). Others would call it *legal conscientious objection*.

8. I avoid gender-specific language by using *conscientious objector*, recognizing that both women and men may conscientiously object to war through worship and teaching activities, nonparticipation in war, public statements, not paying the military portion of taxes, and in other ways. However, thus far all draftees in the USA and Canada have been men.

9. Cf. my essay on "The Credibility of Ecclesiastical Teaching on the Morality of War," in Leroy S. Rouner (ed.), *Celebrating Peace* (Notre Dame: University of Notre Dame Press, 1990), pp. 33-51.

There is a profound difference between abstractly affirming the JWT and applying it accountably to real cases. There are some at-first apparently serious efforts to make the just-war theory relevant by looking concretely at current military options. Yet they end up after all by not saying no at any specified point. This happens in spite of counter-population strategy, nuclear threats, chemical and bacterial warfare, CIA instigating coups and supporting "contras" against constitutional governments, clear-and-destroy tactics against entire populations in rural Vietnam, going to war before everything else has been tried, and disproportionate destruction. Thus they jettison their own credibility by making it inconceivable how they could ever say no in some other case that would be even worse. Cf. the notion of the JWT "without teeth," in appendix 2 (pp. 151-155).

10. James Douglass, in a chapter headed "Anatomy of a Just War," *The Non-Violent Cross* (New York: Macmillan, 1968), pp. 155ff., attempted to challenge Paul Ramsey to admit that the classic just-war criteria, if honestly used, must condemn all modern war and its preparation as well. Ramsey responded in his "Can a Pacifist Tell a Just War?" *The Just War* (New York: Scribners, 1968), pp. 259ff., that if Douglass were consistent, he would not bother with the question.

This exchange was disconcerting not only in its timing (with Ramsey responding to Douglass's argument before it was published) but also in its substance. Douglass intertwined respect for the objectivity of just-war theory with doubts about its honesty and with ambivalence about its concern to moderate a relative justice in a fallen world. It remained unclear whether he thought the doctrine to be a help or a hindrance.

Ramsey in return undermined his own claim for the objectivity of the just-war tradition by his ad hominem claim that a pacifist cannot read it straight. He dodged completely a quite legitimate question, whether an effective no to a particular war on the basis of objective policy criteria was really still possible for him. Ramsey had held that such a no to war was possible in 1961 in *War and the Christian Conscience* (Durham, N.C.: Duke University Press), pp. 151f., and still in 1965 in "Again, The Justice of Deterrence," in *The Just War* (New York: Scribner's, 1968), pp. 314-366, especially p. 357.

Instead of handling this question, Ramsay discussed with great finesse the changes he had or had not made in his thought about the concept of deterrence or about the advisability of legal provision for selective objectors. In so doing, he turned his gaze and thereby that of some readers away from the absence of equally careful attention to refining and institutionally expressing the same criteria applied in the negative case, to declare a war unjust.

11. A lively sample of this kind of movement is the article "A Reluctant Pacifist," contributed by Andrew J. Good, Jr., to *Concern*, United Methodist Board of Social Concerns, Washington, January 1, 1968. Good tries to be honest with Jesus and to safeguard the possibility of ever saying no. He is an honest man with no prior sectarian orientation who finds himself driven to the conclusion that he must begin by saying no now.

Parenthesis: Exceptions and How to Weigh them

1. I have taken this question very seriously, in another study: *What Would You Do?* (Scottdale, Pa.: Herald Press, 1983).

2. Cf. *What Would You Do?* pp. 21ff.

3. This question is separate from the position Gandhi took with regard to the wars fought by the British. Without helping to fight, he did state a moral preference for the British cause, and advocated volunteering for unarmed medical corps service.

4. E.g., Daniel Dombrowski, *Christian Pacifism* (Philadelphia: Temple University Press, 1991). Dombrowski founds everything on the prohibition of taking innocent life, which he finds firmly stated in the church fathers, e.g., Thomas Aquinas, even though in application Aquinas does not follow through consistently. *On War and Morality*, by Robert L. Holmes (Princeton, N.J.: Princeton University Press, 1989), is a more careful presentation of pacifism on a philosophical basis.

5. In this connection the Gospel account of Jesus' "cleansing the temple" may be a helpful corrective. Jesus did no violence; as far as the text is concerned, he used a lash only on the livestock. Yet he did take responsibility for provoking a morally important disorder. Cf. the most

careful reading by Jean Lasserre, "A Tenacious Misinterpretation," in *Occasional Papers of the Council of Mennonite Seminaries and the Institute of Mennonite Studies,* no. 1 (Elkhart, Ind.: Associated Mennonite Biblical Seminaries, 1981), pp. 35-49.

    6. See *What Would You Do?* (note 1, above).

    7. Cf. chapter 18, B, in this book.

3. The Pacifism of Absolute Principle

    1. This reference to the function of a principled statement in the structure of ethical thought is not linked to the linguistic interpretation of a particular statement such as that of the Decalogue. The prohibition of murder, in Exodus 20:13 or Deuteronomy 5:17, did not, then, when those words were first spoken or first written, literally exclude all taking of life, whether we ask about the meaning of the Hebrew word or about the wider context of the Mosaic codes. Yet Jean Lasserre has demonstrated that the capacity of the church to draw general moral guidance from the Decalogue has at no other point been limited by a legal-literal-minimal interpretation of its meaning (*War and the Gospel,* Herald Press, 1962, pp. 165ff., esp. 170f.). Covetousness, false witness, adultery, or idolatry could also be given a minimal ancient-Hebrew meaning in catechesis, but they are not. Therefore, let no one think that the theological-ethical claim made by the pacifist for the sanctity of life is dependent upon a linguistically naive appeal to the Mosaic words, or for that matter to any one particular *wording* of a principle.

    2. Johannes Ude, *Du Sollst Nicht Töten* (Dornbirn, Austria: Hugo Mayer Verlag, 1948).

    3. This is lifted out with special clarity by Geoffrey Nuttall, in the chapter "The Law of Christ" in his *Christian Pacifism in History* (Oxford: Blackwell, 1958; reprinted, Berkeley: World Without War Council, 1971), pp. 15-31.

    4. To distinguish them both from the Ten Commandments and from the "Two Great Commandments" (love of God and neighbor).

    5. Not killing escalates to not hating or deprecating; eye for eye as a restraint on vengeance is replaced by not resisting; loving the neighbor escalates to loving the enemy.

    6. The term *absolute,* which I acknowledge here as the currently prevalent lay term, is misleading. In a lay sense I can use it, as meaning that one does not a priori foresee exceptions to every rule. In that sense it characterizes a position like that of Ude. Yet it would be deceptive if the use of that term were taken to mean denying that there can be dilemmas, or promising that a purely satisfactory choice is always avail-

able. The term *situation ethics*, which occurs here in a taken-for-granted phrasing of 1970, is no longer as familiar. It occurs in a more careful setting in section H of chapter 17 in this book.

7. It is even harder to give a formally legal meaning to the intensified formulations of the Sermon on the Mount.

8. The ecumenical statesman J. H. Oldham, responding to the German bombing of Coventry, spoke categorically against the bombing of civilian populations. Yet he freely conceded that the threshold between unjustifiable and justifiable weapons of war is ambiguous: "I agree that the line is hard to draw; I am sure that there is a line to be drawn somewhere. Christianity has no meaning unless for every man there is a point where he says: 'Here I stand before an absolute: this is unconditionally forbidden' " (*Christian News Letter*, no. 48, September 25, 1940). There are many ways to challenge the axiom that "there must be a line somewhere." Nevertheless, theoretically that axiom still seems to be structurally indispensable to moral communication. This indispensability is not wiped away by saying that the line could be drawn somewhere else, or could bend. The question remains: "Do you ever draw any line?"

4. The Pacifism of Programmatic Political Alternatives

1. The classic statement of Reinhold Niebuhr's critique is his "Why the Christian Church Is Not Pacifist," in *Christianity and Power Politics* (New York: Scribners, 1940). Cf. as well Franklin H. Littell, "The Inadequacy of Modern Pacifism," *Christianity and Society* (Spring 1946): 18ff.

2. Some of the objections to a programmatic approach are those cited above. Another is a form of the objection to principled ethics to which I referred in chapter 3. Somehow the one who rejects pacifism as unfree (Karl Barth, for instance) sees moral bondage in the fact that the act of refusing war is categorical. But that same critic usually does not equally perceive moral bondage in accepting war. To be programmatic may be a vice in pastoral counseling, but there is no alternative in politics.

3. In the midst of the Paris peace talks of February 1969, USA negotiator Henry Cabot Lodge was quoted as warning his counterparts that "violence is no solution." He was addressing himself to the Hanoi/NLF claim that there could be no peace without a new regime in Saigon. Note that this was a struggle in which both parties assumed for decades that violence was a justifiable way to a solution, the organized violence of guerrilla and counterguerrilla war. Even in the mid-

dle of that, it still seemed self-evident and not at all ludicrous to Lodge that a coup d'état or change of regime in Saigon would be wrong because it would "seek to solve a political problem with violence."

4. Note the special claim to realism of Duane K. Friesen in his *Christian Peacemaking and International Conflict: A Realist Pacifist Perspective* (Scottdale, Pa.: Herald Press, 1986).

5. The most serious examples of how this may be done, though on a modest scale, are the study papers which Quakers have addressed to a long series of concrete international problems. They work at real political options with informed seriousness, quite without moralistic short-circuiting of structural issues. Cf. appendix 1 (pp. 145-150).

6. In addition to the literature of the Gandhi and King movements, with their extensive attention to techniques and training, there have been numerous serious studies. In the *Netherlands,* see *Nieuwe Weerbarheid* (Arnhem, 1952) and *Geweldloze Weerbarheid* (Amsterdam, 1965). In the Anglo-Saxon world, note the bibliography of *Peter Mayer, The Pacifist Conscience* (Chicago: Henry Regnery Co., 1967), especially the sections of pp. 442ff. and 451ff. Those who assume as self-evident that violence is the only useful tool have generally not studied this literature. A sample of recently multiplying German literature is the work of Theodor Ebert: *Ziviler Widerstand: Fallstudien . . .* (Bertelsmann, 1971); *Civilian Defence: Gewaltloser Widerstand als Form der Verteidigungspolitik* (Bertelsmann, 1970); *Gewaltloser Aufstand* (Freiburg: Verlag Rombach, 1969). I have left this note in its 1972 form to demonstrate how old and how cosmopolitan is the research field; for an update, see appendix 3 (pp. 157-160).

7. "In the past, most nonviolent struggles have been improvised, without large-scale preparation or training. Thus they may be simply prototypes of what could be developed by deliberate efforts. It seems certain that combination of scholarship and preparation could make future nonviolent struggles much more effective. It is possible that this technique could become a full substitute for violence in liberation struggles and even for national defense": Gene Sharp, in the Foreword, in Monina Allarey Mercado, ed., *An Eyewitness History: People Power; The Philippine Revolution of 1986* (Manila: Reuter, 1986), p. 7. The sources in appendix 3, including several texts by Sharp, validate this projection (pp. 157-160).

8. "As a matter of fact, it is the non-pacifist, not the pacifist, who believes that after a long-drawn-out orgy of indiscriminate killing and wholesale destruction people may be expected to think rationally and act justly. The pacifist has no such confidence in human nature": Er-

nest Fremont Tittle in Arthur and Lila Weinberg, *Instead of Violence* (Boston: Beacon Press, 1963), p. 153.

Political Pacifism: A Semantic Parenthesis

1. Whereas thinkers who call themselves "realist" consider violence to be the definition of the state, others, Karl Barth, for instance, make the cultivation of human community the normative task of the state, with resort to violence being its outer edge, the exception or *ultima ratio.* Cf. Barth's *Church Dogmatics,* vol. III/4, p. 398, or my summary: "Barth's Revision of the Traditional View of War," in my *Karl Barth and the Problem of War* (Nashville: Abingdon, 1970), pp. 37ff.

2. Cf. my "Jesus and Power" in *The Ecumenical Review* 25 (Oct. 1973): 447-454; also in Donald Durnbaugh, ed., *On Earth Peace* (Elgin, Ill.: Brethren Press, 1978), pp. 365-372.

3. Reinhold Niebuhr, *The Irony of American History* (New York: Scribner, 1952).

4. "Aren't you bothered by the equally trivial truth that human affairs—surely precisely because they are in God's hand—on both the small and the large scale—tend with a certain regularity to take some completely different course than had been foreseen . . . because the most important realities of the future, when it has come present, usually rise up so surprisingly that the previously prepared calculation must be crossed out?": Karl Barth, "Letter to an American Churchman, October 1942," in *Eine Schweizer Stimme* (Evangelischer Verlag), p. 289. Those with an ethic of "responsibility" seek to take charge of the course of events for good. But it is a philosophical commonplace that such a position depends for its validity on an idealistically high level of predictive accuracy. See, e.g., my *What Would You Do?* (Scottdale, Pa.: Herald Press, 1983), p. 16; cf. in Alisdair MacIntyre, *After Virtue: A Study in Moral Theory,* 2d ed. (Notre Dame: University of Notre Dame Press, 1984), pp. 70ff., the awareness that "managing," as a part of the liberal social vision, is a fiction.

5. The Pacifism of Nonviolent Social Change

1. Nonviolence understood as an effective tool belongs within the family of the programmatic approaches (chapter 4). I nonetheless describe it separately because of the uniqueness of its picture of peace, its creativity as to method, and its fusing of political concerns that are both personal and structural, interior and foreign.

2. Cf. the argument of Reinhold Niebuhr, in *The Irony of American History* (New York: Scribner, 1952). Yet, as my comments at the begin-

ning of this chapter indicated, a coinciding of pragmatic and principled validations is not a weakness, as long as both kinds of consideration apply authentically.

6. The Pacifism of Prophetic Protest

1. Richard Shaull offered a "reflection" on "The Political Significance of Parabolic Action" at a ceremony where draft cards were turned in, in the context of the University Christian Movement's "Week of Process '67," *Motive* (April 1968): 27f. Shaull indicates awareness that such an approach involves certain kinds of risk, but does not suggest what those risks are, what damage they might do, or how to determine whether they are worth taking.

7. The Pacifism of Proclamation

1. See Philippians 2:12-13.
2. My translation of Hans-Werner Bartsch, "Das Soziale Aspekt der unchristlichen Paranese..." *Communio Viatorum* 5 (1962): 255.
3. The most pointed portrayals of this approach are in the exegetical works of Hans-Werner Bartsch and Dietrich Fischinger: cf. Bartsch's article, "A New Theological Approach to Christian Ethics," in John C. Bennett, ed., *Christian Social Ethics in a Changing World* (New York: Association Press, 1966), pp. 54ff.

Parenthesis: Program and Practicality

1. Except in settings where propaganda has been exceptionally effective, "the people" and "the people in power" may have very different opinions.
2. The reader may note that in 1968 the case of Spock, Coffin, and others changed its character in midstream. It began as an outspoken act of civil disobedience, aiding and abetting refusal to observe the draft, because the laws on that point were deemed unjust. But then it was transmuted into a test case with the claim that the highest law of the land was on the defendants' side.
"The exigencies of a conventional defense against the conspiracy charge often seemed on a direct collision course with the needs of the anti-war movement": Jessica Mitford, *The Trial of Dr. Spock* (Alfred A. Kropf, 1969), p. 173. Cf. William S. Coffin, Jr., and Morris I. Leibman, *Civil Disobedience: Aid or Hindrance to Justice* (Washington, D.C.: American Enterprise Institute for Public Policy Research, 1972).
3. Cf. Speaking Truth to Power, appendix 1 (pp. 145-150).

4. This "ecumenical" or "apologetic" use of casuistics is exemplified by my article on the "what if?" question in my book *What Would You Do?* (Scottdale, Pa.: Herald Press, 1983), pp. 13-42.

8. The Pacifism of Utopian Purism

1. Abraham J. Muste, one of the great pacifist leaders of mid-century, gave currency to this proverb. He however testified that he had first heard it from one "Dr. Schwartz," a veteran of the pacifist wing of the French resistance movement, whom he met in 1945.

2. Social scientists note that utopian social movements bring a critique of pragmatism. Among the studies on utopian societies is Harry W. Laidler, *History of Socialism*, rev. ed. (New York: Crowell, 1969). Social philosophers also see a similar dynamic in worldviews. The hypothetical elaboration of ideal societies is an ancient mode of social criticism.

3. Mark 8:35 and parallels: "For those who want to save their life will lose it, and those who lose their life for my sake, and for the sake of the gospel, will save it."

9. The Pacifism of the Virtuous Minority

1. Cf. a fuller statement of this logic in my "The Constantinian Sources of Western Social Ethics," in *The Priestly Kingdom* (Notre Dame: Notre Dame University Press, 1985), pp. 135-147.

2. These are among the names given by historians to the reform movements most critical of what had become of medieval Christianity: Mennonites, Baptists, Quakers, and many others. Cf. my "Radical Reformation in Ecumenical Perspective" in *The Priestly Kingdom*, pp. 105-122.

3. This is not at all to deny that nonbelievers or believers in something else might be capable of many good works, or that such works might be "good" in very similar ways. But when that happens, such goodness is pure gift, not something we have reason to count on or demand. The obedience of the disciple in the free church is different; it is a covenantal commitment.

4. Here we use the term *virtue* as characterizing voluntary communities; we shall attend later (chapter 18) to its place as a definitional concept in contemporary ethical thought.

5. We shall see more of this dualistic possibility in chapter 16.

6. Cf. below, note 8 to chapter 16, the references to Weigel and Lewy, who have the most respect for the least socially relevant kind of

pacifism. Paul Ramsey and Reinhold Niebuhr also affirmed that kind of respect.

7. Especially is this the case for the views which express the duality geographically or culturally (see chapters 14-16). There is less danger of this when the minority lives amidst the society whose mores it judges, as in the models of St. Francis or the Catholic Worker houses.

8. A capsule vision of the message of this movement is offered by Cornell and Forest in *A Penny a Copy* (New York: The Macmillan Company, 1968).

10. The Pacifism of the Categorical Imperative

1. Luke 6:31: "Do to others as you would have them do to you"; cf. Matt. 7:12.

2. That that other question is also not as simple as it seems, and not as self-evidently a justification of killing, I have spelled out in my book *What Would You Do?* (Scottdale, Pa.: Herald Press, 1983).

11. The Pacifism of Absolute Conscience

1. Cf. Martin Luther at Worms in 1521: "Here I stand; I can do no other."

12. The Pacifism of Redemptive Personalism

1. The phrase "appeal to conscience" is especially prominent in the thought of the Italian Gandhian Lanza del Vasto ("Shanti Das").

2. Gandhi, King, and Lanzo del Vasto would fit in here. However, other strands of their emphasis would also belong under the types in chapters 5, 6, and 9. In the Gandhian movement this concern for winning over the adversary is closely linked with a concern for disciplining oneself (see chapter 17, G). The fasts which Gandhi imposed upon himself were not intended as threats to make the oppressor feel guilty of his suffering or possible death. Instead, they were meant to be self-purgation, because Gandhi and his followers had failed in self-discipline.

3. Cf. especially Geoffrey Nuttall's *Christian Pacifism in History* (Cambridge, Mass.: Blackwell, 1958), pp. 50ff., "The Dignity of Man."

4. Cf. the article "The Wrong Rubicon: LBJ and the War," by Tom Wicker, *Atlantic Monthly* (May 1968), according to which the bombing of North Vietnam was decided upon in one particular conversation between President Johnson and Ambassador Lodge three or four days after President Kennedy's assassination. This article is part of a larger

work on "The Influence of Personality on Politics." This is a further demonstration that personalism is not a peculiar weakness of pacifists. Nothing in the American experience with Panama or the Persian Gulf will change this awareness.

13. The Pacifism of Cultic Law

1. I hasten to point out that other perhaps more widely used, less anthropological understandings of "cult" do not apply at all to the Seventh-Day Adventist communion. It is not esoteric, irrational, manipulative, or anticultural. The quotation at the head of this chapter is from the *Instruction and Information Manual* distributed to Adventist men facing conscription in the 1960s (Washington: National Service Organization, 1964-68, pp. 11-12).

14. The Pacifism of Cultural Isolation

1. In the April 2, 1991, issue of *Gospel Herald*, p. 4.

2. North American Mennonites, especially their Old Order and Old Colony branches and their Hutterian cousins, are probably the most visible and typical example of this kind of pacifism. Yet there are parallels in other traditions (Old Order German Baptist Brethren, Molokans). Many other ethnic-religious groups would take an analogous attitude toward certain doctrinal, cultural, or ethical issues other than that of pacifism. This position differs from that of chapter 16 in that it is taken for granted rather than being argued through.

3. Thus the "mainstream" axiomatic question, "Does this apply to everyone?" (p. 87) is stood on its head.

15. The Pacifism of Consistent Nonconformity

1. "Killing in war . . . calls in question, not merely for individuals but for millions of men, the whole morality, or better, obedience to the command of God in all its dimensions. Does not war demand that almost everything that God has forbidden be done on a broad front? To kill effectively and in connection therewith, must not those who wage war steal, rob, commit arson, lie, deceive, slander, and unfortunately to a large extent fornicate, not to speak of the almost inevitable repression of all the finer and weightier forms of obedience?" Karl Barth, *Church Dogmatics*, vol. III/4 (Edinburgh, 1961), p. 454.

2. See the words of Menno D. Sell at the beginning of chapter 14. Doubts about "dictating Christian morality to pagan governments" contribute as well to the position of chapter 16.

3. The simplest and most widely read case of this misinterpretation is in H. Richard Niebuhr's *Christ and Culture* (New York: Harper, 1951), p. 56, with (his only) specific reference to Mennonites. On this further, see Charles Scriven, *The Transformation of Culture: Christian Social Ethics After H. Richard Niebuhr* (Scottdale, Pa.: Herald Press, 1988), especially pp. 30-48.

Where this reasoning is applicable, it takes culture very seriously. It is precisely because Christ must transform culture that the believing community must manage as much as possible of this world. The stance of consistent nonconformity, reshaping part of the world in a subculture, should not be identified with one Mennonite branch nor with all, as it is a tendency within most branches but not normative in any but the Old Order groups.

4. Cf. the *Christian Century* editorial "The Power, Not the Glory, " May 7, 1958:547.

16. The Nonpacifist Nonresistance of the Mennonite "Second Wind"

1. Scottdale, Pa.: Herald Press, 1944; 3d ed., 1969, 1991.

2. Available in *Church History* (June 1955), in *Mennonite Quarterly Review* 30 (January 1956), and as *The Anabaptist Vision* (Scottdale, Pa.: Herald Press, 1944).

3. The basic source cited by non-Mennonite analysis of Mennonite positions is not the Mumaw pamphlet but rather the chapter "Nonresistance and Pacifism" in Guy F. Hershberger's *War, Peace, and Nonresistance* (see note 1). See reports on the intra-Mennonite discussion in John C. Bennett, *Christian Ethics and Social Policy* (New York: Scribners, 1946), pp. 41ff.; Culbert Rutenber, *The Dagger and the Cross* (New York: Fellowship Publications, 1950), pp. 17ff.; and Thomas Sanders, *Protestant Concepts of Church and State* (Fort Worth, Tex.: Holt, Rinehart & Winston, 1964), pp. 102-104.

4. Sanders, *Protestant Concepts*, pp. 75ff. How widespread this understanding is can be seen in the fact that H. R. Niebuhr (note 3 to chapter 15, above) can take its accuracy for granted, without needing to document or explain.

5. "The basic function of the political order is to maintain order among sinners through the use of coercion. . . . This order is ultimately maintained through police, jails, court, G-men, militia, and armies. All are contrary to strict New Testament standards, though the Bible sets aside all anarchism by sanctioning government for those who do not live on New Testament standards. This is the example, par excellence,

of the necessary evil!" Donovan Smucker, "A Mennonite Critique of the Pacifist Movement," *Mennonite Quarterly Review* 20 (1946): 81ff. For a newer formulation of this position, cf. Daniel Schipani, "An Emerging Neo-Sectarian Pacifism," in John Richard Burkholder and Barbara Nelson Gingerich, eds., *Mennonite Peace Theology: A Panorama of Types* (Akron, Pa.: MCC Peace Office, 1991). These texts make it clear that there is no necessary correlation between this view and cultural obscurantism. Smucker in 1945 and the writers of the 1960s cited by Schipani were among the brightest of their respective generations.

6. This interpretation can appeal to one major strand in sixteenth-century Anabaptist thought, most simply stated in art. 4 of the "Brotherly Understanding" of Schleitheim (February 1527): "The Sword is an ordering of God outside the perfection of Christ. It punishes and kills the wicked, and guards and protects the good. In the Law the Sword is established over the wicked for punishment and death, and the secular rulers are established to wield the same." Here "Law" means the Old Testament; "secular rulers" means civil governments both in the first century and in the sixteenth. When contrasted to "Law" the "perfection of Christ" means the moral resources of the new covenant; when contrasted to governments it means the church.

7. Some Mennonites in fact think the term is a denominational peculiarity. Actually, Mennonites did not use it before the late nineteenth century, since in the German they were using the term *wehrlos* or *defenseless*. One splinter conference body in fact even used *Defenceless* as their denominational name. The term *nonresistance* came into current English usage from Garrison and Ballou, and then from Tolstoy and his many American disciples. Using the term *over against* "pacifism" was a product of the changes described in this chapter, beginning in the 1920s but mostly happening in the 1950s.

8. This Niebuhrian form of backhanded compliment has been renewed by George Weigel in *Tranquillitas Ordinis: The Present Failure and Future Promise of American Catholic Thought on War and Peace* (New York: Oxford, 1989) and by Guenter Lewy, *Peace and Revolution: The Moral Crisis of American Pacifism* (Grand Rapids: Eerdmans, 1988). Both authors describe the pacifism whose integrity they could respect as one which would abstain from any political value judgments.

9. Against the notion that Romans 13 is about war, cf. pp. 205ff. in my *Politics of Jesus* (Grand Rapids, Eerdmans, 1972).

17. And On and On . . .

1. It is not clear who the enemies would be in the kingdom age.

2. Cf. "The Pacifistic Thrust of Anarchism," chapter 18, D, below.

3. For an evaluation from that time, cf. Art Gish, *The New Left and Christian Radicalism* (Grand Rapids: Eerdmans, 1970).

4. Reinhold Niebuhr, *Christianity and Power Politics* (New York: Charles Scribner's Sons, 1940), p. 169.

5. Cf. my passage "The Sword Is Not the Source of Creativity," in *The Original Revolution* (Scottdale, Pa.: Herald Press, 1972), p. 162.

6. Gandhi's strategy fits none of our molds; it fruitfully blended elements of types 4, 5, and 12 as well (see those chapters, above).

7. See type 16, above. Geoffrey Nuttall considers the acceptance of suffering, not for its own sake but as the cost of following Christ, to be most typical of the Anabaptists: *Christian Pacifism in History* (Cambridge, Mass.: Blackwell, 1958), pp. 32ff.

8. Cf. Nuttall's chapter, "The Law of Christ," *Christian Pacifism in History*, pp. 15ff.; and Murray L. Wagner, *Petr Chelčický: A Radical Separatist in Hussite Bohemia*, Studies in Anabaptist and Mennonite History, no. 25 (Scottdale, Pa.: Herald Press, l983), pp. 86ff. His home was at Chelčice in South Bohemia.

18. And Then On and On Some More . . .

1. This is borrowed from fuller formulations used in my teaching.

2. The Maccabees, 167ff. BCE; the Zealot Menahem, 66ff. CE; and the Zealot Bar Kochba, 132ff. CE.

3. Since 1948 the pacifist subculture within Jewry has been shouted down, but its strongest thinkers have not had their minds changed. Cf. Stephen S. Schwarzchild, "Shalom," in *Confrontation* 21 (Long Island University, Winter 1981): 166-176; Reuven Kimelman, "Nonviolence in the Talmud," in *Roots of Jewish Nonviolence*, ed. by Jewish Peace Fellowship (Brooklyn, N.Y.: Revisionist Press, 1984); and "Judaism and Peacemaking," *Fellowship* 42, nos. 1-2 (special issue, Jan.-Feb. 1976).

4. Both Jews and Christians also conversed with and borrowed from Gentile philosophers as well, restating in other words the themes of the sacredness of blood and the unity of the human race.

5. Cited here in one of the simplest forms, from *Non-Violent Resistance* (an anthology of brief texts) (New York: Schocken Books, 1961), pp. 9ff. The theme was frequent with Gandhi.

6. James Russell Lowell, 1819-91, once served the USA as ambassador to Spain and to England; King frequently cited by heart from the poem "The Present Crisis," famed for the first line of the fifth stanza, "Once to every man and nation comes the moment to decide."

7. Some critics have argued that "coercion," obliging the adversary to yield, is the moral equivalent of violence; that whether bodies are broken or blood is shed is not morally the decisive variable. To this Gandhi and King had a threefold answer: (1) They agreed that non-violent action could be unloving, and took measures against that danger. They disciplined their people to maintain respect for the adversary in the midst of conflict. (2) They denied that all forms of "coercion" are morally equivalent. (3) They maintained that the physical integrity of the adversary is an important variable, both tactically and morally.

8. In some ways this view parallels what I called "the long view" in 17, D. Yet here more purposiveness is ascribed to the power behind the course of events.

9. One of King's favorite rhetorical phrases, oft repeated and therefore sometimes modified, was "the arm of the Lord is long [meaning that the mills of God grind slowly], but it bends toward justice." This sounds like Hebrew prophecy or poetry, but it is not clear from what Old Testament text it would have been drawn.

10. Cf. "Anarchic Pacifism," chapter 17, B, in this book.

11. This stance differs from the one escribed in 17, B, which had a pragmatic expectation or promise: by obstruction the present system would be so crippled that other healthier forces ("the people") would spontaneously take over. None of that promise is made by the speculative minds to whom we are here turning.

12. Cf. Robert Paul Wolff, *In Defense of Anarchism* (New York: Harper, 1970).

13. Grand Rapids: Eerdmans, 1987. Eller disregards the ordinary usage referred to above. He delegitimizes all extant power structures but does not describe what would replace them.

14. Grand Rapids: Eerdmans, 1991. Ellul's translator, like Eller, did not respect the usage noted above; *anarchie* in his usage here does not mean anarchy as a social disorder or the total absence of structures, nor does it (as for Eller) represent a Christian position. It designates rather the secular philosophical movement of anarchism as Ellul has encountered it (citing numerous names but not much literature) in France since his youth.

15. Cf. Ellul, *Anarchy and Christianity*, 56ff. Both Ellul and Eller exasperate their critics at this point.

16. This was Ellul's view when he wrote *Violence* (New York: Seabury, 1969), pp. 136ff. The Christian will have to use violence but will know it is sinful. The same is said by William Stringfellow, *An Ethic for Christians and Other Aliens in a Strange Land* (Waco, Tex.: Word Books, 1973), pp. 126ff.

17. There would be other new developments to name, and some of them in fact have been moving in contrary directions. There would be the increasingly abstract debates about what constitutes a convincing argument, and the increasingly nuts-and-bolts study of hard cases in medicine or law. . . .

18. Others characterize this view as "decisionistic" or "quandaristic."

19. Thomas Aquinas, like Augustine and Aristotle from whom he borrowed, was no pacifist. Neither are many of the writers in this vein in the 1980s. To argue that the language of virtue is the best way to talk about the good life does not yet define particular virtues.

20. Notre Dame: University of Notre Dame Press, 1983.

21. Neither patience nor peaceableness figure among the seven normative Thomistic virtues.

22. For Dorothy Day of the Catholic Worker movement, meekness is the virtue of which violence is the opposite vice.

23. Recent interpretations have distinguished the "love" which seeks its own (*eros*), the love which sustains community (*philia*) and the selfless unconditional love which is most like God (*agapē*). Replacing an ethic of ends or means with an ethic of character or virtue does not avoid quibbles about words; it relocates them.

24. In the medieval tradition, which some of the present-day advocates of virtue as a preferred ethical approach pretend to retrieve, it was very important that the several (exactly four plus three) virtues be firmly defined and mapped, with detailed descriptions of how they are divided in categories and how they interlock in life.

It is not clear whether that understanding makes sense today. Nor is it clear that much discussion of whether we have properly understood Aristotle or Aquinas will bring us back to the present more able to make moral sense for our contemporaries.

On the other hand, Hellenistic moral philosophers, and the apostolic writers who freely borrowed from them, enjoyed letting the virtue terms proliferate. Gal. 5:22-23 lists nine, 1 Tim. 6:11 has six, and 2 Pet. 1:5-7 has eight. Only one term appears in all three lists, and only three appear twice.

25. Although the vices which counterbalance the virtues were present in the thought of the Hellenistic moralists, in the New Testament lists, and in the Middle Ages, little has been said about them in the course of the retrieval of virtue language in the 1980s.

19. The Pacifism of the Messianic Community

1. From my own convictions I gather here only those strands which are most relevant to this essay's concern for distinguishing among diverse styles of thought. Most of my vocational effort is invested in interpreting the view of others.

2. Some use the term *incarnation* as a cipher for this commitment to continuing in the world the way of Jesus; in that sense it appears in our chapter heading. It would however lead astray if it were taken to have a clear and necessary meaning. Sometimes *incarnation* is taken to mean Jesus himself; other times it is used to point away from him to the church, or to all of humanity, or to speculations about the metaphysics of his birth.

3. The careful reader will have noted that this description of the difference between the stances of belief and unbelief is different from the dualism of position 16. The messianist continues to proclaim that the call of Jesus is pertinent to those who do not hear it, and even that it has something to say to those who do not trust it entirely. Cf. my *Christian Witness to the State* (Newton, Kan.: Faith and Life Press, 1964).

20. What Have We Learned?

1. The reader will remember that this reproach, addressed to liberal pacifism (4), was exploited particularly by Reinhold Niebuhr, but also by the "neosectarians" (16) and more recently by Guenter Lewy and George Weigel (see note 8 to chapter 16).

Appendix 2: The Spectrum of Nonpacifist Postures

1. Cf. the position of James Childress cited in my *When War Is Unjust: Being Honest in Just-War Thinking* (Minneapolis: Augsburg Fortress, 1984), p. 68.

2. This usage was given currency by Michael Walzer in his book, *Just and Unjust Wars* (New York: Basic Books, 1977).

3. Hugo Grotius, in his landmark argument *On the Law of War and Peace* (1625), picks out Carneades the Cynic as representative of the notion that the only law within nature is self-interest. In *The Prince* (1513; available in various modern editions), the Renaissance court philosopher Machiavelli restated it in a way which remains classical for the modern West.

4. Carl von Clausewitz, *On War* (written 1818-30 and posthumously published); the classical phrase is that "war is the extension of politics by other means." However, since war involves another nation's

territory, it implies the denial that there are criteria above one's own "politics."

5. E.g., by Hans Morgenthau, teacher of political science at Chicago from World War II into the time of the Vietnam War.

6. Randolph H. McKim, *For God and Country or the Christian Pulpit in War Time* (New York: Dutton, 1918), pp. 116-117; as quoted by Ray H. Abrams, *Preachers Present Arms* (New York: Round Table Press, 1933), p. 55; see Abrams's whole chapter on "The Holy War," pp. 50-75.

7. We should acknowledge, however, that in the earlier Western dramas the "good guy" was scrupulously concerned not to shoot first, and to respect women and children. That was closer to the just-war posture. Not all of John Wayne was Rambo.

8. *Just and Unjust Wars* (Harper Collins/Basic Books, 1977), pp. 251-268.

9. This of course assumes, counter-factually, that the suffering population in a situation of rout has some way of influencing the ruler. This same illogic was appealed to in the British argument over city bombing in World War II and in the debate during the 1991 Persian Gulf War.

10. Charles Clayton Morrison, editor of the ecumenical journal *The Christian Century*, whose pacifism had been of the kind that Reinhold Niebuhr excoriated, moved to the "hell" view when World War II began.

Christian Peace Resources

(Notes and appendixes, above, mention additional resources. Also see page 2 for a list of "Related Works by John H. Yoder." All the books below are from Herald Press unless otherwise noted.)

For Serious Study

Aukerman, Dale. *Darkening Valley: A Biblical Perspective on Nuclear War.* Seabury Press, 1981. Herald Press, 1989. Uses biblical stories and motifs to call for resistance to militarism.

Burkholder, J. Lawrence. *The Problem of Social Responsibility from the Perspective of the Mennonite Church.* Elkhart, Ind.: Institute of Mennonite Studies, 1989 [1958].

Burkholder, John Richard, and Barbara Nelson Gingerich, eds. *Mennonite Peace Theology: A Panorama of Types.* Akron, Pa.: Mennonite Central Committee Peace Office, 1991.

Durland, William R. *No King But Caesar?* 1975. A Catholic lawyer looks at the church's attitude toward violence.

Enz, Jacob J. *The Christian and Warfare.* 1972. The roots of pacifism in the Old Testament.

Friesen, Duane K. *Christian Peacemaking and International Conflict: A Realist Pacifist Perspective.* 1986. Proposes that living in a more peaceful world is a realistic alternative.

Gwyn, Douglas, George Hunsinger, Eugene F. Roop, and John H. Yoder, eds. *A Declaration on Peace: In God's People the World's Renewal Has Begun.* 1990. Ecumenical dialogue on peace, war, militarism, and justice.

Hershberger, Guy F. *War, Peace, and Nonresistance.* 3d ed., 1969, 1991. Classic work on nonresistance in faith and history.

Hornus, Jean-Michel. *It Is Not Lawful for Me to Fight*. 1980. Early Christian attitudes toward war, violence, and the state.

Lasserre, Jean. *War and the Gospel*. 1962. An analysis of Scriptures related to the ethical problem of war.

Lind, Millard C. *Yahweh Is a Warrior*. 1980. The theology of warfare in ancient Israel.

Ramseyer, Robert L. *Mission and the Peace Witness*. 1979. Implications of the biblical peace testimony for evangelism.

Swartley, Willard M. *Slavery, Sabbath, War, and Women: Case Issues in Biblical Interpretation*. 1983. Shows how predispositions distort interpretation.

Trocmé, André. *Jesus and the Nonvioleni Revolution*. 1975. The social and political relevance of Jesus.

For Easy Reading

Barrett, Lois. *The Way God Fights*. 1987. The Old Testament "God is a warrior" theme points toward the Gospels of peace.

Beachey, Duane. *Faith in a Nuclear Age*. 1983. A Christian response to war.

Byler, Dennis. *Making War and Making Peace: Why Some Christians Fight and Some Don't*. 1989. Views since Constantine.

Drescher, John M. *Why I Am a Conscientious Objector*. 1982. Issues for Christians facing military involvements.

Driver, John. *How Christians Made Peace with War: Early Christian Understandings of War*. 1988. Shows how Christians up to Augustine gradually became involved in the military.

Eller, Vernard. *War and Peace from Genesis to Revelation*. 1981. Explores peace as a theme developing in the Bible.

Hostetler, Marian. *They Loved Their Enemies: True Stories of African Christians*. 1988. Nonviolent response to conflict.

Kraybill, Donald B. *Facing Nuclear War*. 1982. A plea for Christian witness.

————. *The Upside-Down Kingdom*. 1978, 1990. A study of the synoptic Gospels on affluence, warmaking, status-seeking, and religious exclusivism.

McSorley, Richard. *New Testament Basis of Peacemaking*. 1985. Simple, clear, and sound interpretation by a Catholic.

Miller, John W. *The Christian Way*. 1969. A guide to the Christian life based on the Sermon on the Mount.

Peachey, J. Lorne. *How to Teach Peace to Children*. 1981. Suggestions and ideas for parents.

Ruth-Heffelbower, Duane. *The Anabaptists Are Back! Making Peace in a Dangerous World.* 1991. Stories of those who put their lives on the line in Christian Peacemaker Teams.

Sider, Ronald J. *Christ and Violence.* 1979. A sweeping reappraisal of the church's teaching on violence.

_____. *Non-Violence: The Invincible Weapon?* Word Books, Waco, Tex., 1989. Weighing the effectiveness of nonviolence.

Steiner, Susan Clemmer. *Joining the Army That Sheds No Blood.* 1982. The case for biblical pacifism written for teens.

Stoner, John K., and Lois Barrett. *Letters to American Christians.* 1989. On Jesus, evangelicalism, and militarism.

Wenger, J. C. *The Way of Peace.* 1977. A brief treatment on Christ's teachings and the way of peace through the centuries.

For Children

Bauman, Elizabeth Hershberger. *Coals of Fire.* 1954. Stories of people who returned good for evil.

Dyck, Peter J. *The Great Shalom.* 1990. *Shalom at Last.* 1992. The animals work with the farmer to save their forest home.

Eitzen, Ruth and Allan. *The White Feather.* 1987. Picture storybook on being friends with Indian neighbors.

Moore, Ruth Nulton. *The Christmas Surprise.* 1989. *Distant Thunder.* 1991. Peacemaking Moravians in wartime.

Smucker, Barbara Claassen. *Henry's Red Sea.* 1955. The dramatic rescue of 1,000 Russian Mennonites from Berlin in 1947.

Index

The Author

John H. Yoder is professor of theology at the University of Notre Dame. He has also taught at the Associated Mennonite Biblical Seminaries of Elkhart (Indiana), in the University of Strasbourg (France), in the *Instituto Superior Evangelico* of Buenos Aires, Argentina, and in graduate school short courses in Berkeley, Vancouver, and Melbourne.

Prior to 1965 he served in Europe and North America with the relief and mission agencies of the Mennonite churches.

Other publications by Yoder (in addition to those listed on page 2) have dealt with the areas of Reformation history, missionary methods, church renewal, and the ecumenical movement.

Yoder is a member of the Prairie Street Mennonite Church, Elkhart, Indiana.